a Pilgrim's Guide to Rome and the Holy Land

for the third millennium

a Pilgrim's Guide to Rome and the Holy Land

for the third millennium

Aurelie A. Hagstrom with Irena Vaisvilaite

ThomasMore®
– An RCL Company –
Allen, Texas

ACKNOWLEDGMENTS
Cover design: Demere Henson
Inside design: Melody Loggins of Zia Designs
Cover photos: Jerusalem, courtesy of Biblical Archaeology Society; St. Peter's, the Vatican, courtesy of Andrea Friedman

All Scripture Quotations are taken from the New American Bible, copyright 1970 by the Confraternity of Christian Doctrine, Washington, D.C. Daughters of St. Paul Publishing, Boston, Massachusetts copyright 1976.

All Liturgical Texts are taken from The Sacramentary, English translation by International Committee on English in the Liturgy, copyright 1985 by the Catholic Book Publishing, Company, New York, N.Y.

Send all inquiries to: BOOKSTORES:
Thomas More   Call Bookworld Companies 888-444-2524 or fax 941-753-9396
An RCL Company   PARISHES AND SCHOOLS:
200 East Bethany Drive   Thomas More Publishing 800-822-6701 or fax 800-688-8356
Allen, Texas 75002-3804   INTERNATIONAL:
                                           Fax Thomas More Publishing 972-264-3719

Visit our website at **www.rclweb.com**

Printed in the United States of America

Library of Congress Catalog Card Number: 99-75184

ISBN 0-88347-440-9

1 2 3 4 5   03 02 01 00 99

TABLE OF CONTENTS

Introduction
Open Wide the Doors to Christ

Chapter One
Jubilee Theology, the Holy Year 2000,
and the Third Millennium

Chapter Two
The Christian Tradition of Pilgrimage

Chapter Three
The Pilgrimage to the Holy Land

Chapter Four
The Pilgrimage to Rome

Chapter Five
Traditions and Ceremonies
of the Holy Year

Conclusion
Back to the Beginning, Returning to the Source

DEDICATION

To Miss Leideke Galema and Miss Josefa Koet—
Ladies of Bethany

In Thanksgiving for their Charism of Hospitality
for Pilgrims at the Heart of the Church

*Do not neglect hospitality, for through it some
have unknowingly entertained angels.*
Hebrews 13:2

Introduction

Open Wide the Doors to Christ

 "As the third millennium of the new era draws near, our thoughts turn spontaneously to the words of the apostle Paul, 'When the fullness of time had come, God sent forth his Son, born of a woman.'" (Galatians 4:4)

With these words Pope John Paul II opens his Apostolic Letter, As The Third Millennium Draws Near (*Tertio Millennio Adveniente*)[1]. The event that took place in Bethlehem two thousand years ago has a cosmic significance. The Pope begins his reflection with the notion of time as being fundamentally important in Christianity. The world was created in time and God's plan of salvation gradually unfolds within human history. The coming of Christ in the Incarnation happened in the "fullness of time." And the goal of history is his glorious return at the end of time. From this relationship of God with time there arises a human need to sanctify time, to make it holy.

---

[1]English translation—Origins 24:24 (Nov. 24, 1994). Hereafter referred to as TMA.

11

The words of the blessing of the Easter candle at the Easter Vigil proclaim that Christ is the Lord of time—". . . all time belongs to him, and all the ages. . . ." Jesus is the alpha and omega, the beginning and the end. This means that every year, every day, and every moment are embraced by his Incarnation and Resurrection, and thus become part of the "fullness of time." The person of Jesus Christ is now the horizon of human existence. Time itself is now time in Christ. It is in the context of time and the celebration of anniversaries that the Pope explains the idea and tradition of jubilees.

The Church celebrates various aspects of its relationship to God by remembering the events in the history of salvation. Every Sunday is a remembrance of the Resurrection; every Friday is a meditation on the Passion and Death. On a larger scale, the entire liturgical year is a way of plunging ever deeper into the mysteries of the Christian faith. The cycle of seasons, feasts, and anniversaries enable the Christian community to ponder various events of God's redemptive work. And beyond these rhythms of the liturgical calendar, the Church has designated holy years to remember and reflect upon significant anniversaries of the great events of God's salvation plan. The year 2000 is one such celebration of remembrance and renewal as it marks two thousand years since the Birth of Christ, the Incarnation.

The holy year 2000 has been called by the Pope in the hopes of a "new springtime of Christian life" (TMA 18) in which there would be "an increased sensitivity to all that the Spirit is saying to the Church" (TMA 23). In this way, the Church will be able to enter into the third millennium spiritually renewed. The Pope's primary objective in designating the year 2000 as a special holy year of grace is the "strengthening of faith and of the witness of Christians" (TMA 42). This holy year will not only look back on what God has done in Christ's redeeming Incarnation, but it will also look forward in hope to the fullness of redemption that is the ultimate goal of the Church, indeed of the whole human race.

Pope John Paul II
Courtesy of New Diacolor, Rome, Italy

This holy year of redemption is not simply an anniversary for the sake of Christian nostalgia, but it is a challenge to repentance, renewal, and reconciliation. It is a call for a rededication to prayer, conversion, and witness to Christian faith, hope, and charity as the Church crosses the threshold into the third millennium. "The celebration should confirm the Christians of today in their faith in God who has revealed himself in Christ, sustain their hope which reaches out in expectation of eternal life and rekindle their charity in active service to their brothers and sisters" (TMA 31).

Purpose of this Book

This book is intended to be a guide for pilgrims to Rome and the Holy Land not only during the Jubilee Year 2000, but also into the next millennium. It is meant as a spiritual, historical, and artistic guide. However, it does not purport to be a definitive scholarly text on art history, spirituality, or Church history. There are a plethora of books on the market that fulfill those needs. It is also not strictly a tourist guide, since information will not be given concerning hotels, restaurants, and shops.

Rather, this book is a humble attempt to guide the pilgrim who visits the holy sites and seeks to encounter God in the journey. The information and reflections contained here are simply meant as guides, that is, outlines and indications to help focus the pilgrim on the significance of the traditions, histories and spiritual meanings of the sites. The intention is not to overwhelm the pilgrim with facts, figures, names, and dates. Instead, this book seeks to provide basic information and spiritual reflection that will help the pilgrim to both appreciate the places, art works, and history and to encounter God in the midst of them. In short, it is a guide to enable the pilgrim to marvel and pray, to understand and worship, to perceive and praise.

Aims of the Holy Year

The Jubilee Year 2000 is a period of time in which the Church invites the faithful to participate in special practices and spiritual activities. These practices and activities are meant to revive faith, intensify hope, and stir the faithful to a deeper love of God and others. It is a spiritual renewal that the Church undergoes within the special graces of the holy year, which will hopefully still bear fruit into the future millennium. The celebrations of the Jubilee Year are aimed explicitly at a deepening of the Christian life on all levels— personal, familial, and social, with a view to ongoing transformation.

Such a special period in the life of the Church is also called a "Jubilee," a word of Hebrew origin, which refers to a Jewish festival described in the Old Testament books of Exodus, Leviticus, and Deuteronomy. According to the Law of Moses, every seventh year was to be a "sabbatical year," dedicated in a special way to God. And every fiftieth year was a major jubilee celebration. During a Jewish Jubilee festival, among other things, the earth was to be left fallow, existing debts were cancelled, property was restored to the original owners, and Hebrew slaves were freed.

Catholic tradition, however, has stressed the interior spiritual and religious dimensions of this festival when referring to holy years as "Jubilees." The directives of the Jewish Jubilees were a foreshadowing of the work accomplished by Christ in a definitive way through his redeeming activity. Therefore, the Church has always given special emphasis to conversion, forgiveness of sins, reconciliation, and a renewed celebration of the sacraments when it has called for holy years to be observed.

According to Luke's gospel, Jesus began his public ministry at Nazareth by announcing that he is the fulfillment of the Jewish Jubilee. His mission was to fulfill the prescriptions of the Jubilee as set forth in the prophet Isaiah. "The Spirit of the Lord is upon me, therefore he has anointed me. He has sent me to bring glad tidings to the poor, to proclaim liberty to captives, recovery of sight to the blind, and release to prisoners. To announce a year of favor from the Lord" (Luke 4:18–19; Isaiah 61:1–2). In other words, Jesus is the Jubilee; he personifies this year of "favor from the Lord."

Since Christ is the focal point of the Jubilee, the call of this season of grace is to relationship with Him. Indeed, the primary aim of the Holy Year is an interior call to holiness. A "new springtime of Christianity" is possible only if this relationship with Christ is the source of this renewal. As Pope John Paul II has noted, "Jesus Christ is the new beginning of everything. In him all things come into their own; they are taken up and given back to the Creator from whom they first came" (TMA 6).

The year 2000 is an anniversary of the Incarnation, that is, God becoming a human being in Christ. God has entered the human story, become part of the struggles and triumphs of human life. Christianity has its starting point in the Incarnation of the Son of God, the word made flesh. The celebration of the holy year is a celebration of this fact that God has sought out the human race personally through his Son. "The Jubilee of the Year 2000 is meant to be a great prayer of praise and thanksgiving, especially for the gift of the incarnation of the Son of God and of the redemption which he accomplished" (TMA 32).

Perhaps the best way of describing the objectives of this Holy Year is the two words: renewal and reconciliation. These objectives are directed to the individual lives of every Christian, and then to the life of the Church as a whole. The joy of the Jubilee, according to the Pope, must be based on the forgiveness of sins, penance, and ongoing reconciliation (TMA 33–36).

Where the Jubilee Year is celebrated

One of the unique dimensions of the Jubilee Year 2000 is the places where it is to be celebrated. In the Middle Ages, when the practice of designating of Holy Years began, it was customary to celebrate the Jubilee Year rituals only in the city of Rome. The city of the Apostles Peter and Paul, the visible center of the Church, was the goal of the Jubilee pilgrimage. Pilgrims traveled from far and wide to reach Rome and participate in the holy Year ceremonies and rites.

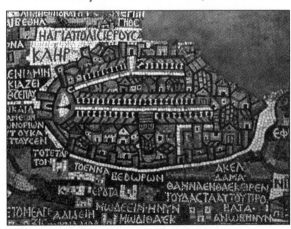

Madaba Map

Courtesy of Biblical Archaeology Society

In the twentieth century, these celebrations have been extended to the local churches throughout the world. Cathedrals and other churches could be indicated by bishops as goals of the Jubilee pilgrimage. Pope John Paul II also encourages the Jubilee celebrations on the local level. But what is new about the Jubilee 2000 is its celebration also in the Holy Land. ". . . the actual celebration of the Great Jubilee will take place simultaneously in the Holy Land, in Rome, and in the local churches throughout the world" (TMA 55). In this way, the Pope integrates the great pilgrimage tradition to the Holy Land into the celebration of the Jubilee 2000. Therefore, this pilgrim's guide will not only focus on Rome, but also on key sites in the Holy Land.

 ## Tradition of the Holy Year Pilgrimage

One of the central holy year practices has always been the pilgrimage. This is more than just visiting the sites of Rome or the Holy Land. It goes beyond mere tourism. A pilgrimage is a journey made in faith, the goal of which is encounter with God. The Jubilee pilgrimage is to be understood within a rich religious tradition. It possesses a high value of sacred symbolism. In the Christian view, life itself is a journey to God, a pilgrimage to the Father's house.

"The whole of the Christian life is like a great pilgrimage to the house of the Father, whose unconditional love for every human creature, and in particular for the "prodigal son" (Luke 15:11–32), we discover anew each day. The pilgrimage takes place

18

in the heart of each person, extends to the believing community and then reaches to the whole of humanity" (TMA 49).

The Jubilee pilgrimage is an outward sign of the inward spiritual journeying to God through the pattern of human living. A religious pilgrimage teaches detachment, imposes sacrifices, and fosters a spirit of loving solidarity with others who are making the same act of devotion. A pilgrimage, when undertaken in the correct spirit of meditation and recollection, stirs up in the heart of the pilgrim a longing for God, a desire for spiritual graces, and a renewed enthusiasm for gospel living.

The pilgrim's instinct is deeply set in the human heart. That is, a pilgrimage is a profoundly anthropological reality. This is the reason why the practice of pilgrimage factors into so many world religions and various cultural traditions. A pilgrimage is a spiritual exercise, which enables the pilgrim to reach out towards God, to deepen the relationship with God, and so to enter into a closer union with him.

The actual journey itself takes on a sacred character, fixing the pilgrim's mind on the divine. It is the intention of the pilgrim which makes the trip a bridge to God. Freed from the distractions of everyday life, a pilgrimage is a form of retreat, that is, putting aside temporarily the duties and preoccupations of daily life and focusing on the things of God. At the same time a pilgrimage can be an act of witness, an outward sign to others of faith, as well as an opportunity of rededication in the pilgrim's own commitment to God.

This book intends to be a simple guide for this kind of trip—a pilgrimage—to either Rome or the key sites in the Holy Land. The information given will hopefully direct the mind of the pilgrim to the deeper significance of the Jubilee pilgrimage, beyond the mere tourism or commercial aspects of it. Instead of a museum, restaurant, or shopping guide, it will provide spiritual guidance for the pilgrim who desires a retreat, and not just a tour.

When discussing the sites of the Rome or Holy Land pilgrimage, special attention will be paid to images. The numerous works of religious art in museums, churches, and monuments are one of the most expressive forms of preaching throughout the history of the Church. Images can inspire, challenge, teach, and elevate the mind and heart of the pilgrim to God. If a picture is worth a thousand words, than one image is worth perhaps more than many volumes of theology. For this reason, much of the on-site information will revolve around sacred images in art.

Holy Door of St. Peter's basilica in Rome
Courtesy of author Dr. Irena Vaisvilaite

Holy sites and religious art are more than museums or artifacts; they maintain a type of

20

living tradition of worship and community. They can be a practical manifestation of the communion of saints, living and in glory. They forge links between the contemporary pilgrim

St. Peter's Square
Courtesy of New Diacolor, Rome

and the living tradition of believers down through the centuries who have visited and worshiped at these important places.

The subtitle of this book is a quotation from Pope John Paul II's very first message to the world after being elected Pope in 1978: "Open wide the doors to Christ." The reason for this is that the opening of the Holy Door in St. Peter's basilica in Rome is the ritual by which the celebration of a holy year is begun and the Church crosses the threshold into the third millennium. This pilgrimage guide seeks to help the reader to "open wide the doors to Christ," the doors of heart, minds, and lives. "Here I stand, knocking at the door. If anyone hears me calling and opens the door, I will enter his house and dine with him, and he with me" (Revelation 3:20).

On another level, the Holy Door of the Jubilee signifies God's mercy and love open wide to all those who seek and ask for it with a sincere heart. The invitation is to cross the threshold and enter fully in communion with God. This guide is a humble attempt to help the pilgrim answer that divine invitation.

ONE

 ## JUBILEE THEOLOGY, THE HOLY YEAR 2000, AND THE NEW MILLENNIUM

Jesus Is Our Jubilee

The Holy Year 2000 is a special Jubilee celebration, which is a spiritual introduction into the third millennium. This anniversary on the Christian calendar marks two millennia since the Incarnation of Jesus. The Jubilee commemorates this key event in God's plan of redemption. It is a special time of joy for Christians as God's tangible coming into the world is celebrated, and their sights are set into the next millennium.

The term jubilee speaks of joy; not just an inner joy but a jubilation which is manifested outwardly, for the coming of God is also an outward, visible, audible, and tangible event . . . the Church rejoices in salvation . . . and she tries to create conditions to ensure that the power of salvation may be shared by all. Hence the year 2000 will be celebrated as the Great Jubilee (TMA 16).

23

The Jubilee of the Incarnation is meant to ponder anew the great mystery of God becoming a human, entering into time and space to bring redemption. Jesus undergoes the most profound self-emptying and takes on human nature. The creator becomes a creature; the supernatural enters into the natural order. "The word became flesh and dwelt among us . . ." (John 1:14).

The Incarnation has been called the "marvelous exchange." God becomes a human so that humans could become God-like. God lowers himself in the Incarnation, so that the human race can be lifted up in glory. God humbles himself so that men and women can be exalted. A paradoxical exchange between humanity and divinity occurs. The Jubilee 2000 celebrates God's gracious initiative and loving presence in the Incarnation. God sends his son Jesus out of sheer love (John 3:16). Jesus, as the fullness of God's revelation, is the very icon of God, reflecting God's glory (Hebrews 1:1–3).

The wonderful mystery of the Incarnation is the heart of the celebration of the Jubilee Year 2000. The center of Christianity is a person, Jesus, the word-incarnate. He is the Jubilee; he personifies God's love, healing, and salvation. The Incarnation is the innovation of Christianity. Jesus is more than simply a prophet, a wonder worker, a moralist, or a great religious leader. He is God himself, speaking and acting to save. And because of his self-emptying in the Incarnation, he is able to elevate human nature and restore humanity's relationship with God (Philippians 2:5–11). This is the cause for a joyful celebration in the Holy Year 2000.

The Old Testament Tradition of the Jubilee Year

Although the Church's celebration of Jubilee Years is not a direct outgrowth of the biblical tradition of the jubilee, it is certainly part of its background. That is, the practice of observing holy years of the Church developed as part of a history of popular devotion in the Middle Ages, and not directly linked to the Old Testament concept of the jubilee. But as these holy years developed in medieval times, a theology of jubilee also was developed that was based, in part, on Old Testament theology. The first Jubilee Year was 1300, but actually the Old Testament theology of jubilee was not a direct part of the explanation of the Jubilee Holy Years until 1350 and beyond.

What is the Old Testament theology of the jubilee which later became the background for the Church's observance of holy years? The jubilee was an institution of ancient Israel which was to be observed on every seventh Sabbath year, that is, after a cycle of 49 years. Every seventh year was a Sabbath year, but after a series of seven of these years (49 years), the Israelites were to celebrate an extraordinary Sabbath year known as a jubilee.

The name jubilee comes from the Hebrew word *yobel,* or "ram," and stands for the ram's horn that was used as a type of "trumpet" which was blown to inaugurate the jubilee year. The ram's horn was blown on the Day of Atonement in the Jewish calendar, a day of repentance and reconciliation (Exodus 19:13). Therefore, the Day of Atonement was the appropriate solemn feast on which to begin the jubilee year (Leviticus 25:8ff). On a deeper level, the Hebrew word *yobel* is a synonym for the Hebrew word *deror*, meaning "liberty or release." This deeper meaning reflects the economic, social, and spiritual liberty of the jubilee observance. The jubilee was a year of release and forgiveness on many levels.

Observance of the jubilee was to include the return of land to its rightful owners, a release of slaves, and a rest from planting and harvesting. The legislations for this observance are based on the law codes found in Exodus 21–23, Leviticus 25, and Deuteronomy 12–26. Jubilee legislations drew upon the principal themes of slave release, agriculturally fallow years, loan interest, cancellation of debts, land repurchase, and land restoration, as found in these biblical texts. By returning properties, canceling debts, freeing slaves, and letting the land to lie fallow, the ancient Hebrews were invited to undergo a complete transformation of society on human, moral, economic, social, ecological levels. During the jubilee, the Israelite community was given an extra-ordinary sabbatical year in which to reorder their priorities and re-orient themselves to their covenant with God.

There is a question as to whether or not this custom was ever observed. That is, there is no solid historical evidence that the jubilee year was ever celebrated in ancient Israel. The Bible contains no evidence of the historical observance of the jubilee year. This silence would suggest, therefore, that these jubilee laws and legislations were not enacted as part of public policy in ancient Israel. Nevertheless, these jubilee customs and observances remain an ideal for community life recognizing God's sovereignty and the need for social justice in light of the covenant with God.

The prescriptions for the jubilee year remained an ideal, and prophets in Israel, such as Isaiah later elaborated this ideal. Isaiah saw the jubilee concept as an ideal that would become a reality in the mission of the Messiah who was to come. The future kingdom of the Messiah would include all of the elements of the jubilee, come to their fruition. The Messiah would bring an experience of release, restitution, and freedom for all who trusted in God. This "year of the Lord's favor" was the image Isaiah used to demonstrate how the future-coming Messiah would bring the definitive jubilee (Isaiah 61:1–2). Thus the prophets held onto the idealized institution of the jubilee as a vision of hope for release, forgiveness, and social justice in God's future reign.

The Pope's Theology of the Jubilee

In *As The Third Millennium Draws Near* (TMA), Pope John Paul II recalls this great biblical tradition of how jubilee years were celebrated in the Old Testament. The Pope quotes passages from the biblical books of Exodus, Leviticus, and Deuteronomy, which give the prescriptions for the Hebrew jubilee. The Old Testament jubilee was to be a combination of prayer, worship, charity, and social justice. It was meant both a celebration of the people's covenant with God and a challenge for deeper conversion and adherence to the precepts of the covenant.

The Pope notes that the Old Testament jubilee was marked as a holy year to be consecrated to God, which included release from debts, liberation of slaves, justice concerning ownership of land, and a period of rest for animals and fields, reminiscent of the great rest of God on the seventh day of creation. This solemn sabbatical year of the jubilee was to happen every fiftieth year. The themes of the biblical jubilee were, in short, freedom, release from bondage, emancipation, reconciliation, justice, and equality among all members of the Hebrew community.

The jubilee year was meant to restore equality among the children of Israel, offering new possibilities to families which had lost their property and even their personal freedom . . . Justice according to the law of Israel consisted above all in the protection of the weak . . . the foundations of this tradition were strictly theologically linked first of all with the theology of creation and with that of divine providence . . . the jubilee year was meant to restore this social justice" (TMA 13).

The Pope also emphasizes that Jesus brought himself the biblical tradition of jubilee to completion himself. Jesus as God's Messiah ushers in the "year of the Lord's favor" (Luke 4:16–30). All of the biblical traditions and customs of the jubilee find their fulfillment in the ministry of Jesus. Through his saving words and deeds, Jesus brings the blessings of the jubilee to their fruition.

"The jubilee, 'a year of the Lord's favor,' characterizes all the activity of Jesus . . . The words and deeds of Jesus thus represent the fulfillment of the whole tradition of jubilees in the Old Testament" (TMA 11–12).

With the life, teachings, ministry, as well as the climactic Death and Resurrection of Jesus, the jubilee is accomplished. Jesus is the true jubilee gift of the Father, though the pouring out of his Spirit. Jesus brings this jubilee to perfection simply because he himself is the jubilee. His life and mission is considered to be the "center of history" by Christians.

The Incarnation, Death and Resurrection of Jesus are not the center of history in a chronological sense. Obviously, the events of his historical life do not stand at the chronological middle of the spectrum of human history. Rather, Jesus is the center of history because his life, death, and resurrection give meaning and purpose to all of human history. The Christ event gives salvific meaning and value to human history. All of the events of human history are now evaluated in light of the person of Jesus and his mission. This is a theological principle. The Christ event is like a fount or fountain of meaning, purpose, and value for all other aspects of human history.

The centrality of the mission, death, and resurrection of Jesus is due to the fact that in him is the fullness of God's revelation. God's self-disclosure to the human race find its definitive apex in Jesus (Colossians 2:9). The Christ event is unrepeatable, once and for all, and yet it is the never-ending source of salvation for all. It is like a fountain that can be drawn from by all peoples of all times. This is the why the Christ event is the "center of history" and Jesus is the Lord of history, according to Christian belief (TMA 5).

Development of the Jubilee Holy Years in the Life of the Church

As mentioned above, the Jubilee celebrations in the Middle Ages were not a direct outgrowth of Old Testament theology. Although the term "jubilee" was used in inaugurating these holy years, the theology of the holy years only gradually came to embrace the Old Testament vision of the jubilee. Where and how, then, did the tradition of calling holy years "jubilees" originate?

Some of the earliest references to Church celebrations which used the term "jubilee" were related to a certain pilgrimage in Medieval Rome. Pope Innocent III in 1208 A.D. began an institution in Rome that was called a "jubilee." This jubilee consisted of a religious procession with the veil said to be that of Veronica containing the image of Christ. "Veronica's Veil," a precious relic in medieval Rome, was carried in solemn procession through the streets of the city from the basilica of St. Peter to the Church of the Holy Spirit. This "jubilee procession" occurred on the Sunday after the Octave of the Epiphany.

This relic of Veronica's Veil was believed, according to Christian popular tradition, to contain the image of Christ, made as Veronica wiped his blood-smeared face, as he carried his Cross on his way toward Calvary, where he would be crucified. Although not a Biblical story, this tradition of Veronica became very widespread. The author Dante records that religious pilgrims made the journey to Rome to see this image of Jesus which he left as an example of his face. This jubilee pilgrimage which was started by Pope Innocent III reflected a popular movement in religious piety of his time. In the thirteenth century, there was a growing devotion to the humanity of Jesus. The preaching, teaching, and theology of that time focused on the fact that Jesus was truly human. This emphasis on the humanity of Jesus made God in some ways more "accessible" to common people, who could relate to Jesus in his likeness to them. The public display of Veronica's Veil in Rome was a way of revealing this sacred humanity in a tangible way. For many pilgrims at this time, seeing the veil was the primary reason for making the journey to Rome.

The original use of the term "jubilee," then, was linked to the procession in Rome with this relic of Veronica's Veil during the Christmas Season. The Christmas season is a time for the Church to ponder anew the mystery of the Incarnation. It is interesting that this original jubilee was so closely tied to the mystery of the Incarnation, as is the Jubilee Year 2000. God became a human, and this mystery was the focal point of the solemn procession with the image of Jesus' humanity on Veronica's Veil.

"Saint Veronica"
by Hans Memling
National Gallery of Art, Washington, DC
Courtesy of Edizione G. Quarta, Rome

31

The Incarnation is a doctrine that claims that God has been "seen," experienced, touched, and heard in Jesus. And the pilgrims to Rome during the Middle Ages wanted to "see" God through the image of Jesus' face on Veronica's Veil. It was a way of somehow entering into the mystery of the Incarnation more profoundly.

"What was from the beginning, what we have heard, what we have seen with our eyes, what we looked upon and touched with our hands, concerns the Word of life—for the life was made visible; we have seen it and testified to it . . ." (1 John 1:1–2).

Jesus, in the Incarnation, is the face of God. He has been called the icon of God, the true image of the Father. In the Old Testament, it was said that no one could ever look upon the face of God and live. Even Moses could not look upon God's face (Exodus 33:20). But when Jesus becomes a human, now God is visible. "No one has ever seen God. The only Son, God, who is at the Father's side, has revealed him" (John 1:18).

The jubilee procession in Rome, and the later holy years during the Middle Ages, which were called jubilees, kept up the devotion to the humanity of Jesus through Veronica's Veil. The "face of Jesus" on the cloth relic was publicly displayed at St. Peter's basilica usually on Sundays during the jubilee holy years. In fact, the souvenir which medieval pilgrims carried back to their own countries was the image of the "Holy Face," a small metal badge or a painted likeness of the image on Veronica's Veil. This medieval souvenir summed up the purpose of their journey to Rome.

The Jubilee Year Indulgence

 By definition, an indulgence is linked to the jubilee themes of release, reconciliation, and forgiveness of sins. How did the theological concept of indulgence become a part of the medieval jubilee years? It seems that this practice actually goes back to the procession with the Veil of Veronica begun by Pope Innocent III in 1208 A.D. This pilgrimage to Rome and participation in the procession benefited the pilgrim spiritually through the acquisition of an indulgence for the forgiveness of sins. This responded to the needs of the popular piety of the day, which placed a great emphasis on indulgences. A certain widespread sense of guilt influenced greatly the piety of pilgrims and their desire to receive the profound forgiveness which an indulgence offered.

Penitential practices were popular during this time because of the desire of Christians to obtain forgiveness of sins. The practices of giving alms, performing works of mercy, and making pilgrimages were some of the ways that the faithful practiced penance. This devotional penitential movement seems to be part of the motivation for the jubilee pilgrimage with Veronica's Veil and the obtaining of remission of sins.

The very first holy year in 1300 A.D., called by Pope Boniface VIII, is connected to this devotional penitential movement present in the Church at that time. Large numbers of pilgrims crowded into Rome near the end of the year 1299 A.D. under the impression that a special indulgence was being offered for the centennial celebration. Actually, the Pope himself was unaware of any practice of granting special indulgences at the end of each century. So, the Pope ordered the records to be searched, and although no documentary evidence could be found to support the popular conviction, he granted this spiritual favor to pilgrims to Rome.

Pope Boniface VIII granted the fullest pardon of sins to any penitential pilgrim who visited the basilicas of St. Peter and St. Paul and made a full confession of sins. Thus the tradition of the jubilee year indulgence was started. Medieval artists and writers recorded the historic event in inscriptions and paintings.

Fresco by Giotto of Pope Boniface VIII proclaiming first holy year, St. John Lateran, Rome
Courtesy of author Dr. Irena Vaisvilaite

A contemporary inscription with the text of Pope Boniface's proclamation may still be seen over and to the left of the Holy Door in St. Peter's basilica. And in the basilica of St. John Lateran, there is a fresco by Giotto showing the Pope publicly reading out the document which proclaimed the event.

Pope Clement VI called the next holy year in 1350 A.D. This jubilee year was specifically linked to the Jewish practice of the jubilee in ancient Israel. The Pope drew a connection between the Old Testament jubilee practice and the new Christian jubilee, to be celebrated every fifty years in

34

Rome. And as time went on, this jubilee year theology developed. The basis for these celebrations was to be found in the Old Testament Jewish traditions of jubilees, and yet the popular devotional penitential aspect of pilgrimages to Rome was always kept.

The jubilee year indulgence was understood as a Christian version of the themes of release, forgiveness, and reconciliation of the Jewish jubilee. The jubilee year indulgence focused on the great redemption won by Christ and now available to all for the remission of sins. The conditions for receiving this great pardon of the indulgence were gradually developed and included pilgrimage, penance, confession of sins, and receiving Communion.

Pope John Paul II, in TMA, has also highlighted the importance of release and remission of sins in connection with the jubilee year 2000 indulgence.

> . . . a year of remission of sins and the punishments due to them, a year of reconciliation between disputing parties, a year of manifold conversions and of sacramental and extrasacramental penance. The tradition of jubilee year involves the granting of indulgences on a larger scale than at other times.

Contemporary Theology of Indulgences

What exactly is an indulgence and how is the celebration of the holy years linked to them? As mentioned above, the granting of indulgences was part of the Veronica Veil pilgrimage in Medieval Rome. And it was a desire for a full remission of sins on the part of the pilgrim crowds in 1299 A.D. that prompted Pope Boniface VIII to call the first holy year in 1300 A.D. However, this theology of indulgences has not always been properly understood. Indeed, it has sometimes been an unfortunate cause of misunderstanding of the Catholic theology of redemption.

This was especially true during the Middle Ages when there were abuses of the practice of granting indulgences. Disgracefully, in the 15th and 16th centuries, the preaching of the indulgences made it thought that, thanks to more or less important donations, one would be able to obtain eternal salvation without true interior conversion or confession of sin. It was this kind of erroneous preaching and the offer of indulgences for money that was the occasion that gave way to the Protestant Reformation. That is, much of the reasoning for the Reformation on the part of Martin Luther was due to an abuse of indulgence theology.

Since the theology of indulgences has often been misunderstood in the past, it is important for the preaching and teaching of the Jubilee Year 2000 indulgence to be clear so as to prevent further false understandings. Technically speaking, indulgences are the remission of temporal punishment of a sin already pardoned. This pardon of sin, first of all, comes through the Church through the "power of the keys" granted to it by Jesus himself (Matthew 16:19; 18:18; John 20:22–23). This sacramental power of forgiveness of sins is present in the Church through the power of the Holy Spirit and is not a human work at all. The sacrament of Penance or Reconciliation is a gift of God for release, forgiveness, and healing.

Once sin has been forgiven or pardoned through the sacrament of Reconciliation, there is still a rupture or a disorderedness in the human person's relationship with God. Although the sin has been forgiven, there still remains a further step of ongoing healing. This "remnant of spiritual disorder" has traditionally been called temporal punishment and its remission has traditionally been called an indulgence. The sin is definitely forgiven, and yet a deep interior renewal of the person is still needed. This deep conversion is a process that continues throughout the Christian life. The journey of conversion consists in a pattern of recognition of sin, contrition, repentance, forgiveness, and ongoing personal renewal and healing.

The traditional language of indulgences is an attempt to explain this ongoing process of spiritual healing of sin and its side effects in the spiritual life. The ripple effects of sin include disorder, alienation, and lack of love for God and others. Not only must sin be eradicated and forgiven, but its ripple effects must also be addressed. This is done through personal penitential practices such as prayer, fasting, almsgiving, and pilgrimage. This might be seen as an "ongoing rehabilitation" of the human heart. And this is what the traditional language of indulgences is all about. An indulgence is a kind of interior "medicine" for the spiritual woundedness that results from sin.

The beginning and foundation of any indulgence is an authentic conversion to God through Jesus in the power of the Holy Spirit. This is what it means when it is said that the granting of an indulgence confirms the spirit of conversion. Any indulgence presupposes a reforming penance through the sacrament of reconciliation and actions like works of mercy, fasting, alms giving, prayer, and pilgrimage. An indulgence is a grace obtained through the concrete exercises of faith, hope, and charity. It is meant to reorder one's relationship with God and also to repair the defects of disorder caused by sin.

The Jubilee Year indulgence, that has been a part of the holy years since 1300 A.D., is an extraordinary opportunity for conversion and renewal of heart. A Jubilee Year celebration seeks to create conditions and opportunities for the faithful to receive deep spiritual healing and reconciliation. The Church desires to stimulate and assist this never-ending process of growth in holiness through the offering of a special indulgence, known as a plenary indulgence during the Jubilee Year 2000. In a sense, the Jubilee Year is a way of drawing from the fountain of the richness of God's grace and the salvation won through Jesus' death and resurrection. And the traditional language of indulgences is an attempt to illustrate this salvific activity.

The preaching and teaching of the Jubilee 2000 indulgence seeks to encourage and develop the deep and lasting reform of hearts and renewal of life with the aim of reconciliation of the human race with God and with one another. The jubilee indulgence is an opportunity for healing of the consequences of sin. One aspect of this healing that the jubilee indulgence highlights is the deep mystery of ecclesial participation in Christ's salvation. This mystery is known as the Communion of Saints. It is the reality of spiritual solidarity among all members of the faithful, past and present.

According to Catholic theology, those who have died, marked with the sign of faith, can assist and cooperate in the process of redemption of those in this life who are still "running the race of faith."

> *Therefore, since we are surrounded by so great a cloud of witnesses, let us rid ourselves of every burden and sin that clings to us and persevere in running the race that lies before us while keeping our eyes fixed on Jesus, the leader and perfecter of faith (Hebrews 12:1–2).*

This cloud of witnesses is the Communion of Saints. Through the mysterious influence of the sanctity, prayers, and example of this Communion of Saints, it is possible for the members of the Church here on earth to grow spiritually and be transformed into Christ's image. The spiritual solidarity of the Church on earth and in heaven can produce the fruit of holiness, which manifests itself in faith, hope, and charity. In fact, the healing and interior remedy offered by an indulgence depends on this spiritual solidarity, this cooperation among the members of the Church, past and present, through prayer, example, and sanctity. The great cloud of witnesses, the Communion of Saints, is an inspiration, example, and source for conversion, healing, and rehabilitation from the profound effects of sin.

The theology of indulgence then, is about salvation, transformation, and justification. It is about becoming more and more Christ-like. It concerns recognizing the roots of sin, purging sin through the sacrament of Reconciliation, and being healed of the debilitating remnants of sin. Indulgences are a means of being purified of the effects and attractions of sin in order to be able to see God clearly. The medieval pilgrims to Rome wanted to "see God" on the Veil of Veronica in the image of Jesus' face. Through purification of sin and its remnants, it is possible to see God and to be like Him.

> *Beloved, we are God's children now; what we shall be has not yet been revealed. We do know that when it is revealed we shall be like him, for we shall see him as he is. Everyone who has this hope based on him makes himself pure, as he is pure (1 John 3:2–3).*

"Veronica" by El Greco, Museum of Santa Cruz, Toldeo, Spain
Courtesy of Spanish Ministry of Culture

Vision of the Jubilee

At the beginning of this chapter it was stated that Jesus personified the Jubilee. He is the source of healing, liberation, and salvation. He proclaims and ushers in the "year of the Lord's favor." In Luke 4:16–30, Jesus proclaims in the synagogue sermon at Nazareth that he is the

Messiah who is the herald of God's jubilee. Reflecting on the prophecy of Isaiah 61, Jesus announces that his mission is to touch all of human life with his redemptive work. He will heal, free, and redeem people, meeting them in their deepest vulnerabilities and greatest pain. In this way, all manner of evil is broken, and the inauguration of the Kingdom of God becomes possible through him. Jesus announces the advent of God's reign and the defeat of the powers of evil and the tyranny of sin in all its forms. And the language that he uses is that of the jubilee year.

> *The spirit of the Lord is upon me, because he has anointed me to bring glad tidings to the poor. He has sent me to proclaim liberty to captives and recovery of sight to the blind, to let the oppressed go free, and to proclaim a year acceptable to the Lord . . . Today this Scripture passage is fulfilled in your hearing (Luke 4:18–19, 21).*

The jubilee is realized, that is, made present and fulfilled, in the person and work of Christ. So, the jubilee is not a plan, a program, or a project. It is a person, the person of Jesus Christ, Son of the Father, and Savior and Redeemer of humanity. That is why the holy year is always an invitation to meet Christ, to encounter his saving grace and redemption. The good news to the poor, the release of prisoners, the recovery of sight for the blind, and the freedom promised to the oppressed are all metaphors for the salvation which comes through the forgiveness and profound healing of sin effected through faith in the crucified and resurrected Lord. The "year of the Lord's favor" comes in him.

The holy year is a channel of grace, a type of quasi-sacramental. The Jubilee Year 2000 is an outward celebration of an inward grace, that is, relationship to Christ. The jubilee is an invitation to ponder anew the mystery of the Incarnation where the face of God is revealed to the world through Jesus, the icon of the Father. It is not simply an invitation for nostalgia. Jesus is not to be encountered simply as an historical figure of the past. Rather, the Jubilee is an encounter with the living dynamic Lord of history.

One of the resounding themes of TMA is the Scripture passage from Hebrews 13:8, "Jesus Christ is the same yesterday, today, and forever." It serves to clearly define the vision of the Jubilee 2000 and third millennium, which is the absolute centrality of the person of Christ. He is the center of history and the eternal source of salvation. The mysteries of the Incarnation and Redemption can never be exhausted. The power and saving dynamism of these mysteries are what the Church invites the faithful, and indeed the world, to enter into, not only during the holy year celebrations, but on into the future. In other words, the invitation is to meet Christ, who is the same yesterday, today, and forever. The Jubilee Year call is to open wide the doors of human hearts to Christ in the new millennium (Revelation 3:20), for he is the Jubilee.

TWO

THE CHRISTIAN TRADITION OF PILGRIMAGE

Encountering the God of the Journey

One of the ancient Christian spiritual traditions is the experience of pilgrimage. A pilgrimage is a pilgrim's journey or, a view of mortal life as a journey. The pilgrim is one who travels to a sacred place as an act of religious devotion or, on a deeper level, journeys to a future life—an afterlife. A pilgrimage is not just any trip; it is a trip with a religious intent. The pilgrim is a person who has a religious intention for going to a sacred place or a holy site as an act of religious devotion. In some way, the person making a pilgrimage is fulfilling a religious duty or satisfying a religious desire. It is the destination and the spiritual intention of the pilgrim which gives the pilgrimage its special character. Before a pilgrim starts the trip, his or her intention is clear—they are going to meet the divine in some way through this physical traversing of distance.

A pilgrimage is not just a journey to get from point A to point B. It is a spiritual trip with an interior dimension. The phenomenon of pilgrimage is found in almost every culture on earth, and in nearly every world religion. In the religion of Islam, Moslems make a pilgrimage to Mecca, and in Judaism, Jews go to Jerusalem as an act of devotion. Since the very first holy year in 1300, the notion of pilgrimage has been part of the jubilee practices. Where did this tradition originate? How is it to be observed for the Jubilee 2000? And what is the meaning of the experience of pilgrimage in the Christian life?

Pilgrimage and the Holy Years

As mentioned in Chapter One, the first use of the term "jubilee," in regard to a devotional practice in Rome, seems to have been the jubilee procession with Veronica's Veil in Rome started by Pope Innocent III in 1208 A.D. Medieval pilgrims flocked to the city of Rome for this devotional event. And when the time for the jubilee procession was approaching at the end of the year 1299 A.D., the city was flooded with pilgrims seeking a special indulgence from the Pope in light of the centennial celebrations. It was this ground swell of the faithful and the desire for a special plenary indulgence that prompted Pope Boniface VIII to proclaim the first holy year.

The pilgrimage to Rome to see the precious relic of Veronica's Veil thus became the devotional foundation for the beginning of the holy year celebrations. It was this pilgrimage, a long-standing devotional and penitential practice, that was the basis for the very first holy year in 1300 A.D. This explains why the experience of pilgrimage has been such an important part of the celebrations of holy years since the very beginning. In a way, Pope Boniface VIII's proclamation of the holy year "institutionalized" the ancient pilgrimage to Rome which had been part of the devotional heritage of the Church since the days of the early Christians.

As the holy years continued, and as the theology of the jubilee developed, the idea of the pilgrimage took on new meanings and deeper significance. What began as a private devotional practice became a call to all the faithful to enter into the holy year fully. Indeed, the Rome pilgrimage was seen as the way of observing the holy year. The pilgrimage eventually became described as a way to show devotion to the Apostolic founders of the Church of Rome, St. Peter and St. Paul. And later in the Middle Ages, the Rome pilgrimage became linked to a biblical motive. The biblical theology of redemption was described as the reason for the journey to Rome because the holy year pilgrimage was later seen as a way of encountering Christ, the Redeemer and Savior.

 ## The Theme of Pilgrimage in the Bible

The Christian theme of pilgrimage finds its origins in the Hebrew theology of pilgrimage in the Old Testament. The ancient Israelites observed pilgrimage as a devotional practice. They had special shrines and places of worship, which were pilgrimage centers. As early as the Patriarchs, Abraham, Isaac, and Jacob, the Old Testament records the marking of sacred space as an important part of their encounters with God.

During their travels throughout the land of Canaan, Abraham, Isaac, and Jacob often came across the sites of Canaanite idolatrous worship, and they were motivated to re-consecrate these places to the God of Israel. They entrusted these ancient sacred sites such as Shiloh, Gilgal, Shechem, Mamre, and Bethel, to the care and the veneration of succeeding generations. The Old Testament books of Exodus, Leviticus, and Deuteronomy contain the prescriptions and laws concerning the ancient Hebrew practice of pilgrimage to these holy places.

For the ancient Israelites, pilgrimage was a devotional practice which sought to provide a mystical encounter with God. Eventually, during the reigns of King David and King Solomon, the city of Jerusalem became the destination for the most important pilgrimages. Jerusalem was the political and spiritual capital of the nation and became known as the city of God, Mount Zion. The magnificent Temple built by King Solomon was the spiritual heart of the city because it housed the Ark of the Covenant. The Ark was the most sacred object of ancient Israel because it contained the tablets of the Law given to Moses by God on Mount Sinai.

Pilgrimage to the central sanctuary in Jerusalem became the hallmark of the Israelite religious experience from the time of Kings David and Solomon. The book of Deuteronomy prescribes three annual pilgrimages. A journey to Jerusalem was part of the observance of the feasts of Passover, Pentecost, and Tabernacles. The destination of these pilgrimages was the Temple where offerings would be made to God.

Three times a year, then, every male among you shall appear
before the Lord, your God, in the place which he chooses: at
the feast of Unleavened Bread, at the feast of Weeks, and at
the feast of Booths. No one shall appear before the Lord
empty-handed, but each of you with as much as he can give
in proportion to the blessings which the Lord, your God, has
bestowed on you (Deuteronomy 16:16–17).

This theme of pilgrimage is also found in the New
Testament. Jesus himself was a pilgrim. As a young boy he accompanied his parents, Mary and Joseph, to Jerusalem for the feasts
(Luke 2:41–52). And as an adult, Jesus fulfilled the prescriptions
of the Law by observing the pilgrimage festivals in Jerusalem. All
four gospels recount Jesus' journeys to Jerusalem. And after the
Ascension of Jesus back to heaven, the Apostles continued to
observe the pilgrimage customs of Judaism. It was during the
feast of Pentecost in Jerusalem that they received the power of the
Holy Spirit and began their preaching ministries (Acts of the
Apostles 2:1–11).

Pilgrimage Practices of Early Christians

In the earliest days of the Church, Palestine was a
destination for pilgrimage. The motivation for these
journeys was devotional. The early Christians wanted to visit and
venerate the sites where Jesus had lived and labored during his
earthly ministry. As early as the second century A.D., there is
evidence of pilgrims visiting the place of his birth in Bethlehem,

the sites of his ministry in Galilee, and the places of his Passion and Death in Jerusalem.

Visiting these sacred places was not merely an act of nostalgia for Christian pilgrims. Rather, it was a meditative encounter with Christ in their midst. Their desire was that they would come closer to Christ as they engaged in their devotional processions, prayers, and practices at these holy sites. The past was recalled at the places where these events of salvation history happened, in order to draw out their meanings for the present. Pilgrims sought spiritual nourishment in their meditative remembrances. They wanted to encounter Christ in the present, and so to be transformed by him.

A great impetus was given to Christian pilgrimages to Palestine in the days of the Emperor Constantine and his mother Helena in the fourth century A.D. After the legalization

Basilica of the Holy Sepulchre, Jerusalem
Courtesy of Holy Views, Ltd

of Christianity in the Roman Empire by Emperor Constantine in 313 A.D., his mother Helena traveled to the Holy Land to see the places associated with the life, Death, and Resurrection of Jesus.

She and her emperor son had basilica churches built on the sites of the Birth of Jesus in Bethlehem, and the site of his Death and Resurrection in Jerusalem. These basilicas became important centers of pilgrimage, and although remodeled and rebuilt over the centuries, they still remain holy sites today for modern Christian pilgrims.

Rome—The City of Peter and Paul

Besides the pilgrimage to the Holy Land, it became customary very early in Christian history to visit the "threshold of the apostles," *ad limina apostolorum.* This is a reference to the tombs of the martyred apostles Peter and Paul in Rome. The Roman cleric Gaius in the second century A.D. claimed: "I can show you the trophies of the apostles, if you will go as far as the Vatican or the Ostian Way, you will find the monuments of those who founded this Church." These "trophies" were markers at the graves of the apostles which were places of pilgrimage for the early Christians.

The ancient monuments, artwork, and inscriptions give evidence of a steady stream of early Christians pilgrims to Rome. With the edict of Emperor Constantine in 313 A.D. legalizing Christianity, a new impetus was given to devotional visits to the eternal city of Rome. The main focus of pilgrimage was the tombs of St. Peter and St. Paul, over which Constantine built basilicas. These two joint founders of the Church of Rome were venerated together on a special feast day of June 29, which is still on the liturgical calendar as the feast of Peter and Paul.

Other churches, which Constantine built, were the Holy Cross in Jerusalem basilica, St. Agnes basilica, St. Lawrence basilica, and St. John Lateran basilica. Pope Damasus, bishop of Rome in the late fourth century A.D., began the proper care of the catacombs as sites of pilgrimage by adding signposts and markers to help pilgrims find their way around in order to venerate the tombs of the martyrs.

In the years that followed after the edict of Emperor Constantine, numerous pilgrims flooded the city of Rome from east and west. Pilgrimage to Rome was perceived as an act of devotion, and a demonstration of reverence for the apostles St. Peter and St. Paul. These two apostles and their martyrdoms were understood as the foundation for the Church of Rome and the reason for its place of honor among all the other important ecclesial sees of the world such as Jerusalem, Antioch, Alexandria, and eventually Constantinople. The bishop of Rome took on the responsibility of "guardian" for the trophies of the apostles, the tombs, which were the holiest sites in Rome.

4th century A.D. marble profile of St. Peter and St. Paul, Paleo-Christian Museum, Aquileia, Italy
Courtesy of Tipolito Giusti, Rimini, Italy

50

The early pilgrims to the eternal city were referred to as "romerus," "romipeta," or "romarius" (later on as national languages developed: "romeo" and "romipeto" in Italian, "romieu" in French "romeria" in Spanish, "romeiro" in Portuguese) Hence, the English verb "to roam" has its origins in the experience of the early Christian pilgrimage to Rome.

In the year 638 A.D., the Moslem conqueror Caliph Omar seized Jerusalem. The city was no longer controlled by Christians. And with the Moslem expansion in the East in later centuries, a great number of pilgrims were prevented from travelling to the Holy Land. This culminated when fanatical Moslems burned the Constantinian church of the Holy Sepulchre to the ground in 1010 A.D. Because of the relative inaccessibility of the Holy Land, Rome became the chief destination of Christian pilgrimages. Europe became isolated from the Holy Land because of poor travel conditions, poor communication, and political factors. Rome, therefore, became known as another Jerusalem, or the "second Jerusalem." Just as the ancient Israelites made pilgrimage to Jerusalem, Mount Zion, so now Christians journeyed to Rome, the new city of God, symbol of the heavenly Jerusalem.

During the Medieval Holy Years, the papal call for pilgrims to come to Rome for the jubilee celebrations often used the imagery of the new Jerusalem. Rome was the new Mount Zion and pilgrims were exhorted to approach the city in the same jubilant mood of the Israelite pilgrims drawing near to God in ancient Jerusalem.

Rome was the site of martyrdom not only for St. Peter and St. Paul, but also for hundreds of other early Christians who gave the ultimate testimony of their faith in Christ through the shedding of blood. The graves of these martyrs were also locations of pilgrimage. These sites, often in the Catacombs, would be visited especially on the anniversary of the death of the martyr. This was considered the martyr's "birthday," *"dies natalis,"* a birth into eternal life. Eventually the Eucharist was celebrated over the graves of these martyrs. The ceremony included the reading of the account of the martyr's trial and death at the hands of the Roman Empire, and then readings from Scripture. In this way, the memory of the martyr was preserved and was proposed as an example for the faithful to follow.

Dome of St. Peter's basilica, Rome
Courtesy of New Diacolor, Rome

The jubilee year pilgrimage proclaimed by Pope Boniface VIII in 1300 A.D. included only two basilicas, the church of

St. Peter in the Vatican, and the church of St. Paul on the Ostian Way. Constantine built these churches over the tombs of the apostles, as mentioned earlier. However, as the traditions of the holy year pilgrimage developed, other churches were added to the Roman sojourn. Eventually, pilgrims during the holy year celebrations observed the custom of visiting the additional churches of St. John Lateran and St. Mary Major. Even today, these are the four churches to be visited to fulfill the jubilee year Roman pilgrimage. And later the so-called "minor basilicas" were also informally part of the pilgrimage: Holy Cross in Jerusalem, St. Sebastian, and St. Lawrence. At times, the church of St. Mary in Trastevere was also a destination of the jubilee pilgrimage.

 ## Modern Pilgrimage and Religious Tourism

In modern times, long-distance travel has become faster, more frequent, more comfortable, and more efficient. It seems that the modern traveler does not face the same dangers, inconveniences, and difficulties as their ancient counterparts. It may appear that the modern experience of pilgrimage contains none of the penitential aspects that the ancient and medieval pilgrims faced. Does this mean, then, that a modern pilgrimage is not an act of devotion? How does the phenomenon of tourism fit into the holy year traditions of religious pilgrimage?

The phenomenon of modern travel and tourism is a human phenomenon, and every human experience can also be a religious experience. Every human situation has the potential for being a religious encounter. This is because God has entered into the human experience through the Incarnation. All of reality can now be a channel of the divine. Material reality has been infused with the presence of Christ. Therefore, authentic human experiences can be a means of encountering God. In this way, a human situation such as travel or tourism can potentially be a situation that opens the mind and heart to things divine.

Tourism can, if carried out humanely and in a Christian spirit, contribute to the development of a spirit of reconciliation. Tourism promotes contacts among believers of various religions and nonbelievers. And, if filled with the spirit of charity and hope, tourism can actually become a forum or means for ecumenical dialogue.

Travel can also offer other possibilities of reconciliation. Through it, families are sometimes reunited and dialogue is reopened. Family members who had been separated for long periods of time are now able to be free from the constraints of schedules, work, and other responsibilities in order to spend time with one another. A type of reacquaintance occurs which can lead to deeper bonds of love and openness with each other, in short, reconciliation.

Besides family reconciliation, travel and tourism can facilitate meetings among peoples of different backgrounds and cultures. This can result in societies being transformed, other cultures being appreciated, and friendships being formed across traditional boundaries. Since travel always has a specific destination, tourism allows places which had not been previously known and perhaps not made use of, to be appreciated, treasured, and loved, as gifts of God, the creator of all good things.

Perhaps most importantly, in light of the jubilee year pilgrimage, tourism can actually be a form of evangelization. As a cultural activity, tourism can be an effective form of evangelization especially for the modern traveler. This is true because religious tourism offers one of the most expressive forms of preaching, that is, preaching through images. Artistic images can preach in a way that reaches the human heart more effectively, at times, than the spoken word.

The numerous works of religious art in museums, temples, and monuments, can inspire, challenge, and lift the heart of the modern traveler to God. This type of "preaching," however, requires an adequate spiritual and cultural formation of the one acting as the guide of the tour. A properly trained guide can use these evocative images as a means to foster the religious character of the tour or pilgrimage. Art treasures can be illustrated from a spiritual point of view as a means of evangelization.

The phenomenon of modern religious tourism, if accompanied by proper pastoral activity, can become a type of "incarnational evangelization." That is, the art and material realities encountered on the trip can be a means, a "material cause," of encountering God and others. By encountering artistic images, very often the image of God is revealed, not only in the material artworks, but also more importantly, in other people. This can actually open the way for conversion of heart and reconciliation with God and others. Religious tourism can be a form of spiritual care. By admiring the works of the Creator, it provides spiritual insights and leads, ultimately, to the glory of God.

Of course, even modern tourism has its difficulties and disappointments. Although modern technology has certainly made travel easier and more comfortable, there are also inconveniences and at times obstacles encountered during any journey. And it is here, it seems, that the penitential aspect of pilgrimage might be experienced. The relations among travelers, the demands of the schedule, and the realities of foreign cultures can, in their own ways, contribute to the penitential dimensions of a pilgrimage. If these logistical and personal difficulties are accepted not as distractions, but as part of the journey experience, than even these disappointments can be used to raise the mind to God and foster a spirit of penance and reconciliation, in short, a true spirit of pilgrimage.

The Contemporary Experience of Pilgrimage

The Church considers pilgrimage to be one of the privileged means of raising the mind and heart to God. Even with the conveniences of modern life, pilgrimage is still a spiritual activity, as discussed above. There are certain human dimensions of a pilgrimage that can be profound opportunities for spiritual experiences.

All travelers or pilgrims have some similar feelings and experiences that can be opportunities of the Spirit. One feeling or experience is great anticipation in the days and weeks before this trip, and a sense of adventure that is manifested both before and during the trip. The "explorer side" of the pilgrim anxiously awaits the sights, sounds and adventures of the pilgrimage.

Another feeling often experienced by travelers or pilgrims is feeling out of control. Pilgrims are not in control as they are at home since someone else is planning the schedules, meals, activities, and accommodations. Actually, by having others plan these aspects of the pilgrimage, the pilgrim is freed up for other activities like sight seeing, touring, shopping, photography, praying at the shrines and visiting the holy sites. The anxious feelings about the details of the trip, the schedule, and logistics are part of the spiritual abandonment of the pilgrim. And, if properly advised, this restlessness and worry could be channeled into more creative activities such as prayer, contemplation, or sightseeing and photography.

"Sacred Way" from the Roman Forum, Rome, Italy
Courtesy of New Diacolor, Rome

Another typical feeling a pilgrim or traveler experiences is being overwhelmed with newness. There comes a moment when all the pilgrim wants to do is to "stop" to absorb a little of what has been seen and heard. Even though time is usually provided for that, it never seems like enough. Many travelers keep a journal or diary to record their thoughts, impressions, and feelings, and then once back at home, they can take time to ponder what was seen and heard and experienced during the pilgrimage.

What all this means is that while the pilgrim is journeying in planes, in buses, on trains, or by foot, there is also an inner journey unfolding. This inner journey may or may not correspond with what is going on each day on the itinerary. Each person's pilgrimage is unique and occurs more in the heart than on a bus or in an airplane. Whatever feelings are experienced, it is important for the pilgrim to keep in mind that that God can work through those feelings and speak to the heart during a pilgrimage. The pilgrim moves out of familiar environments and familiar routines, in order to get in touch with the deepest pilgrimage, that of the human heart.

Liturgically, the Church includes prayers for pilgrims and their journeys in its traditions of blessings. A special celebration for the blessing of pilgrims at their departure and on their return is provided by the *Orders for the Blessings of Pilgrims* (National Council of Catholic Bishops, Book of Blessings, New York: Catholic Book Publishing Company, 1989, pages 259–270) and should definitely be used for any pilgrimage.

The Order for the blessing of pilgrims on their departure and upon their return includes respective introductory rites, a pastoral reflection, Scripture readings, intercessory prayers, and a final blessing appropriate for the occasions. The pastoral reflection for the departure of pilgrims states:

Brothers and sisters, as we set out, we should remind ourselves of the reasons for our resolve to go on this holy pilgrimage. The place we intend to visit is a monument to the devotion of the people of God. They have gone there in great numbers to be strengthened in the Christian way of life and to become more determined to devote themselves to the works of charity. We must also try to bring something to the faithful who live there: our example of faith, hope, and love. In this way both they and we will be enriched by the help we give each other.

And the prayer of blessing on their departure states:

All-powerful God, you always show mercy toward those who love you and you are never far away for those who seek you. Remain with your servants on this holy pilgrimage and guide their way in accord with your will. Shelter them with your protection by day, and give them the light of your grace by night, and, as their companion on the journey, bring them to their destination in safety. We ask this through Christ our Lord.

After the pilgrimage is completed, upon their return home, the pastoral reflection states:

Our pilgrimage has been a privileged period of grace given to us by God. We who have come in trust to this holy place are moved with a new resolve to be renewed in heart. The sanctuaries that we have visited are a sign of that house not built with hands, namely, the Body of Christ, in which we are the living stones built upon Christ, the cornerstone. As we return home, let us live up to the vocation God has given us: to be a chosen race, a royal priesthood, a holy nation, a people God claims for his own, so that we may everywhere proclaim the goodness of him who called us from darkness into his marvelous light.

The prayer of blessing upon return is:

Blessed are you, O God, Father of our Lord Jesus Christ. From all races of the earth you have chosen a people dedicated to you, eager to do what is right. Your grace has moved the hearts of these, your friends, to love you more deeply and to serve you more generously. We ask you to bless them, so that they may tell of your wonderful deeds and give proof of them in their lives. We ask this through Christ our Lord.

 ## The Jubilee 2000 Pilgrimage

For the first time, the destinations for the holy year pilgrimage have been expanded. Pope John Paul II has declared that not only will the holy year take place in Rome, but also simultaneously in the Holy Land and in the local churches (TMA 55).

Since the experience of pilgrimage has been expanded, everyone in the Church has an opportunity to make a pilgrimage in observance of the Jubilee Year 2000. First and foremost, the Jubilee celebrations should take place in the local churches. The preferential destination is the cathedral of the diocese because of its well-known significance as the center of the Christian community. However, other churches and shrines may be determined by the local bishop or bishops' conference as goals of pilgrimage. The final goals of pilgrimage for the universal church are the city of Rome and the Holy Land. Those places in the Holy Land remind the pilgrim of the Birth, Life, Death, and Resurrection of Christ. And Rome is the site of the *ad limina apostolorum,* the threshold of the tombs of the Apostles Peter and Paul.

The Christian Journey

The experience of pilgrimage has a deep value of sacred symbolism. It suggests that life itself is a spiritual journey, and it teaches detachment, imposes sacrifices, fosters solidarity, and produces charity. A pilgrimage requires, and can also stir up, enthusiasm, religious ardor, and piety. The motivation for a pilgrimage, and the spirituality which inspires it, are some of the highest expressions of piety in Christian experience. A pilgrimage teaches that the Christian has no permanent place on earth. Rather, the entire people of God is on a journey to the heavenly city. "For here we have no lasting city, but we seek the one that is to come" (Hebrews 13:14).

The journey motif is an evocative symbol of the spiritual quest of the Christian. The Christian is an "alien or an exile" in this world (I Peter 2:11). Earthly life is therefore to be considered as an "exodus," a constant movement or migration of faith. Abraham is the Old Testament representative figure of the spiritual pilgrim. The Exodus of the Hebrews from Egypt is also a paradigm for the Church, which journeys not to Mount Sinai, but rather to the heavenly Jerusalem (Hebrews 12:22). The application of the Exodus image to the Church shows that God is to be encountered as the God of the Exodus, the God of the journey.

A pilgrimage is a type of "retreat on the move." It is a symbol and a source of growth in discipleship. In the Old Testament, the same Hebrew word *derek,* is used to signify a road or way and also, by extension, *derek* is used to describe a "way of life." The pattern for the Christian journey has been set by Jesus himself. He opens the way through his death and resurrection. In fact, one of the earliest designations of the Christian community was "the Way," (Acts of the Apostles 24:14). And, in a similar vein in the New Testament, Jesus is called "the Way" (John 14:6). All of these images stress that the Christian is one on the move, on the way, pressing forward, asking new questions, seeking new truths, experiencing new life.

To be a pilgrim is to have an opportunity to reorder priorities, refocus perspectives, and look to the future. It can be an adventure in faith like that of Abraham, who left security and certainty for the spiritual quest with God. Abraham had an uncertain destination, and yet he trusted God, who had uncertain blessings in store for him (Genesis 12:1–3). A pilgrim is one who tries to follow Abraham's example of faith and obedience by recalling the God of the journey who leads, guides, and blesses. In this way the pilgrimage fosters a self-surrender and openness to God who can rekindle dreams, fulfill hopes, and renew lives. The physical traversing of distance during a pilgrimage becomes a symbol of the heart's desire to approach God in trust and abandonment.

As the Pope states:

The whole of the Christian life is like a great pilgrimage to the house of the Father, whose unconditional love for every

*human creature, and in particular for the "prodigal son"
(Luke 15:11–32), we discover anew each day. This
pilgrimage takes place in the heart of each person, extends to
the believing community and then reaches to the whole of
humanity (TMA 49).*

The observance of the ancient tradition of pilgrimage
enables Christians to leave the distractions of daily life and seek
the God of the journey. A pilgrimage to Rome, or the Holy Land,
or to the local cathedral or shrine is not simply an exercise in
nostalgia. It is not an attempt to recapture the past. Rather, it is a
way of encountering God in the present and receiving spiritual
consolation. The heart of the pilgrim, often dried out by the
demands of work and the drain of consumerism, can be nourished
and filled with the healing graces showered by God during the
journey. Then the mind is freed up for pondering deep spiritual
questions, questions that often are buried under the busyness and
perpetual motion of daily life. It is then that a "new evangelization" of mind and heart can occur. And the renewed pilgrim can
walk in the way of the Lord, who is himself the Way, the Truth,
and the Life. *Were not our hearts burning within us as he spoke to
us on the way?* (Luke 24:32)

THREE

 ## THE PILGRIMAGE TO THE HOLY LAND

Reading the Fifth Gospel of the Holy Land

The Jubilee 2000 is the first holy year in the history of the Church which includes Jerusalem and the Holy Land as destinations for the holy year pilgrimage. The Pope states:

> *The actual celebration of the Great Jubilee . . . will take place simultaneously in the Holy Land, in Rome, and in the local churches throughout the world (TMA 55).*

In the past, the city of Rome was the only pilgrimage site for the holy years. Gradually the holy year celebrations of modern times included the local churches throughout the world. But this is the first time that the Holy Land is part of the focus of the celebrations.

The three major faiths of western civilization regard the Holy Land as their own religious cradle. To the Jews it is the land of the sacred Torah; to Christians that of the Old and New Testaments; and to Moslems it is Abraham's country—they also claim him as patriarch through his son, Ishmael. These religions claim that the land itself is holy, because major events in the history of salvation occurred there. In some way, Jews, Christians, and Moslems have encountered God at the sacred sites of this land.

For Christians, the Holy Land is a kind of "fifth gospel." Much as the four canonical gospels, Matthew, Mark, Luke, and John, witness to the saving events in the life, death, and resurrection of Jesus, the Holy Land is a physical, tangible witness to these events. Salvation history is recorded in the very soil, rock, and water of this land. Since the early days of Christianity, there has been a keen interest in tracing the footsteps of Jesus and recording them for posterity. The early Christians journeyed to the places sanctified by Jesus the Christ, who had taught, healed, suffered, died, and rose there. A devout pilgrimage to the Holy Land became a fifth gospel, an encounter with the life and ministry of the Lord through the sites, sounds, and experiences of the place where eternity had once entered into time.

 ## The Theology of the Land

The history of the Jewish people, as recorded in the Old Testament, begins with the call of Abraham to leave his people and his land and to serve the one God in a new land, the land of Canaan.

"The Lord said to Abram: 'Go forth from the land of your kinsfolk and from your father's house to a land that I will show you'" (Genesis 12:1). The rest of the Old Testament becomes the story of Abraham's descendants and the land given to them by God. In fact, the promise of the land by God becomes a central motif in this story.

In common English usage, the word land refers to a wide range of physical realities. Land can be dirt, rocks, and sand. Land is the ground producing vegetation, the field for farming, and the topsoil of the earth. Land is a place for humans to build shelters and cities. Land is the domain between the boundaries that separate countries. Land is that area of the earth bounded by oceans. Land is *terra firma*.

Land is not just a physical reality, either. The notion of land also refers to social realities. From one culture to another, or even within a culture, land can have different sociological meanings. Land is a social symbol with a range of meanings. For the people of the Old Testament, land was a sacred thing. In the Old Testament, there is a deep "sense of place," the land was a "sacred space."

The people of the Old Testament had a deep sense of the sacred space of the land, because they saw God as intimately bound up with this land. The land is God-given. As mentioned above, in the context of the covenant God makes with Abraham, the land is promised (Genesis 12:1–9). God calls Abraham, and Abraham makes a migration. Abraham is an immigrant in this land of Canaan, there are already people living there. And throughout the Abraham cycle of stories, Abraham has various dealings with these people.

In Genesis 12:6–9, Abraham journeys by stages. While he is on the move, Abraham establishes some sacred shrines and places. These scenes show Abraham symbolically claiming ownership of the land (Genesis 12:8, 13:14–18). These sites bind Abraham's seed to the land, because at these sacred locations, the God of the ancestors is to be found. In this chartered land, the ancestors, the patriarchs, find their God. The land promise by God to Abraham and his descendants is ratified in a solemn treaty or covenant in Genesis 15:7–21.

In the book of Exodus, Moses is reminded of the promises to Abraham. At his call scene at the burning bush, God identifies Himself as the God of Abraham, Isaac, and Jacob. And God repeats the land promise to Moses (Exodus 3:5–10). And after the plagues, the Red Sea event, and the Sinai event, the wandering Hebrews finally arrive at this Promised Land. God has delivered them from Egypt and slavery, as he promised, and the fulfillment of God's promise to Abraham back in Genesis, "the Promised Land" is realized.

The book of Joshua is a fulfillment of the promise made to Abraham—the promise of the land of Canaan (Genesis 17:4–8). It gives a glorious picture of the conquest of the land. It is a glorious re-statement of the theme that God had given Israel this land. The traditions in Joshua remember events associated with the taking of the land.

In these Old Testament stories, the land is always described as "flowing with milk and honey." According to the ancient worldview, milk and honey in abundance were the blessings of paradise. Throughout the Old Testament, the land is described in this way. To nomadic tribes who wandered in the barren desert, Canaan was a veritable paradise. The land was part of the creedal confession of Israel—all of these events are theologically and historically connected—Exodus, Sinai, and the conquest of the land (Deuteronomy 6:20–23; 26:5–9).

The promise to Abraham in Genesis 12 had two parts—numerous descendants and the land. Even in the earliest Israelite literature, it is evident that the importance of the land for the lasting identity of the people was recognized. The traditions of the Patriarchs—Abraham Isaac, and Jacob, and the Exodus story witness to the fact that the Israelites knew that their permanent identity was assured only when the land bore the name of the people. It is a common theme of the book of Deuteronomy that the land is the gift of God. The phrase: "the land which the Lord your God gives to you" is almost a cliche in the book (Deuteronomy 6:10–12). The theology of Deuteronomy also teaches that the retention of the land is conditional upon the fidelity of the people to the law of God—they will keep the land only if they are obedient to the covenant. In fact, the land is not inert; it offers an opportunity and a challenge. Besides speaking of "possessing the land," the Scriptures also speak of "walking in the ways of the Lord" (Deuteronomy 8:6), or listening to God's voice" and of "heeding and fulfilling all the words of the law" (Deuteronomy 17:19). Land, people, and the law are inextricably bound up together.

Israelite Pilgrimage Tradition

Since the land was considered to be sacred by the Jewish people, the tradition of pilgrimage arose as part of their religious identity. This phenomenon was closely linked with the tradition of holy places, theophanies, or traditions and stories, which held the memory of events that happened in the lives of key Old Testament figures. Even during the times of the Patriarchs, references to pilgrimages are made. Abraham, Isaac, and Jacob, during their travels throughout the Promised Land, often came across pagan sites of idolatrous worship, which they reconsecrated and claimed for the God of Israel. These sites were entrusted to the care and veneration of succeeding generations. The books of Exodus, Leviticus, and Deuteronomy collect and develop this ancient practice of pilgrimage to holy places and give legislation concerning this practice. These religious laws attempt to develop piety and worship as well as a sense of religious, social, and historical unity of the people of Israel.

The Old Testament legislation for pilgrimage stresses not only the devotional aspect or mystical experience of pilgrimage, but also the social and moral importance of pilgrimage. Pilgrimage to the sacred sites is not only an occasion for thanking God for graces and blessings, but it should also be an occasion to feel more intensely the divine and sacred significance of history.

With the entrance of the Jewish people into the land of Canaan under Joshua, and the division of the land among the twelve tribes, the pilgrimage tradition continues in two separate directions. The ancient shrines of the patriarchs, like Bethel, Shiloh, and Shechem continue to be places of worship and the destinations of pilgrimage, although sometimes confined to one tribe. On the other hand, once the magnificent city of Jerusalem had been built and the Temple completed during the "golden age" of Kings David and Solomon, Jerusalem itself becomes increasingly the religious center for all the people. Jerusalem, city of David, city of God, becomes the political and spiritual heart of the nation (2 Samuel, I Kings).

In 2 Samuel, one of King David's first actions after conquering Jerusalem was to transfer the Ark of the Covenant to his new capital. The Ark, the sacred chest containing the tablets of the law brought down from Mount Sinai by Moses, had been previously kept in Shiloh, the central sanctuary of the twelve tribes. The King himself took on the cultic and political responsibility of moving the ark.

"Then David, girt with a linen apron, came dancing before the Lord with abandon, as he and all the Israelites were bringing up the ark of the Lord with shouts of joy and to the sound of the horn" (2 Samuel 6:14–15).

The Ark symbolized God's presence in the midst of his people. By transferring it to a permanent location in Jerusalem, King David made it the heart of his city; God's holiness was now bound to a place. The Temple built for the Ark by David's son Solomon became the house of God, the Lord's dwelling in the midst of his chosen people. When the building of the Temple was completed, King Solomon officiated at the dedication ceremony and the Ark of the covenant was placed in the inner sanctuary of the Temple, the "holy of holies," as it came to be called (1 Kings 8:1–66).

Jerusalem now became the sole destination for pilgrimage, since it was both the political and spiritual heart of the nation. Jerusalem became the "holy city," the city of Zion, city of God, a focus for profound emotions of piety, devotion, ardent longing, and theological symbolism. The history of the Temple became identified with the history of Jerusalem, and indeed with the history of the entire Jewish people.

Eventually, the ideas of God's covenant with his chosen people, the promised land, the city of Jerusalem, the Temple, and the chosen house of David merged into one integrating symbol (Isaiah, the Psalms, Jeremiah 31:34–39; 33:14–26). Throughout the rest of the Old Testament, the rise and fall of Israel can be traced by the rise and fall, the destruction and rebuilding of Jerusalem and the Temple. For example, the most severe judgement of God on Israel is the Exile, the destruction of the Temple, the ruin of Jerusalem, and the loss of the Promised Land (2 Kings 25:1–21). Jerusalem acquired not only historical, but also existential significance.

After the Exile in Babylon, the people who returned to Jerusalem rebuilt the Temple under the leadership of Ezra and Nehemiah. The practice of pilgrimage was then re-established with even greater fervor. Psalms 122 and 126, for example, reflect this enthusiasm for making a pilgrimage to the sacred city. It was during this time that the legal and religious norms of the pilgrimage to Jerusalem took definitive shape. For example, pilgrimage was suggested to be made three times a year if possible, and the financial offering for the Temple was introduced. Special arrangements were made for pilgrims who were usually given hospitality by the people of Jerusalem.

Jerusalem in the Vision of Jesus

Jesus' life, ministry, death, and resurrection are profoundly grounded in this theology of Jerusalem from Jewish tradition. As an infant, Jesus was brought to Jerusalem, to the Temple, to be presented to the Lord, according to Luke 2:21–40. As a child, he journeyed to Jerusalem with his parents Mary and Joseph, probably to make his bar mitzvah in Luke 2:41–52. After being lost for three days, his parents find the boy Jesus in the Temple astounding the scribes and teachers of the law with his wisdom. As an adult, Jesus himself traveled to Jerusalem for religious pilgrimage in observance of certain feasts (John 5:1; 7:10; 12:12), including the Passover. For Jesus and his disciples, Jerusalem and the Temple were the most tangible symbols of Judaism.

Jesus predicts his death at Jerusalem in the passion predictions of the Gospels (Mark 8:31; 9:31; 10:32–34 and parallels). When he thought his time had come, Jesus resolutely "set his face" toward Jerusalem and began the journey which would end in his death (Luke 9:51). Jesus' mission reaches its climax at Jerusalem. His triumphal entrance into the city marks the beginning of the end for Jesus. He will spend the last week of his life preaching, teaching, and healing in Jerusalem, and specifically in the Temple (Matthew 21:23 and parallels).

One of the most dramatic prophetic actions of Jesus occurs in the Temple. Jesus' cleansing of the Temple (Mark 11:17 and parallels) was a symbolic action that pointed to his own body as the new temple, not made by human hands (Mark 14:57; John 2:13–22). Jesus himself becomes the locus of worship. The fact that he replaces the Temple and its sacrificial worship is strikingly clear at the moment of his death, when the veil in the Temple separating the outer courts of the Temple from the holy of holies is torn in two, from top to bottom (Mark 15:38; Matthew 27:51; Luke 23:45).

Old City of Jerusalem as seen from the Mount of Olives

Courtesy of Holy Views, Ltd

Jerusalem is the site of the apex of Christian salvation history, namely, the death, resurrection and Ascension of Jesus. His first Resurrection appearances in the Gospels are in Jerusalem (Luke 24; John 20). And his Ascension takes place near Jerusalem (Luke 24; Mark 16). And in Jerusalem, his first followers gathered in prayer to await the promised Holy Spirit who would form the Church at Pentecost (Acts of the Apostles 1–2).

Christian Tradition of Pilgrimage

Christian believers began travelling to the Holy Land fairly early in the history of the Church. The first of whom seems to have been Melito, bishop of Sardis, who journeyed to the Holy Land to confirm the canon of the Christian Old Testament as early as approximately 172 A.D. About 212 A.D., Bishop Alexander appeared in Jerusalem to pray there and visit the holy sites of the life of Jesus. Even the ancient Christian theologian Origen is reported to have retreated to the Holy Land after fleeing his opponents in Egypt at the beginning of the third century A.D. The first written Christian pilgrimage account is from an anonymous 4th-century pilgrim from Bordeaux. Soon after comes the written account of Egeria, a late-4th-century aristocratic pilgrim from Spain, who gives a much fuller account of the sights and experiences of the Holy Land.

But it was not until the Roman Emperor Constantine ended the persecution of the Christians and legalized Christianity in 313 A.D., that the stream of Christian pilgrims to the Holy Land became a flood. After his conversion to Christianity, Constantine initiated an ambitious building program of churches in Rome and in the Holy Land. Constantine built Christian basilicas in honor of Jesus, the Apostles, and early Christian martyrs.

In the Holy Land, Constantine's attention focused first of all on three sacred sites: the site of the Birth of Jesus in Bethlehem, the site of the tomb of Jesus in Jerusalem, and the site of the Ascension of Jesus on the Mount of Olives. He built magnificent basilicas at these places so that the events of salvation history might be memorialized and represented so that Christian pilgrims might enter into these saving events more profoundly. This was more than just an exercise in nostalgia, this was a way for Christian pilgrims to relive and mystically enter into the events of salvation history. This building campaign of Constantine witnesses to a growing sense of the sanctification of place in the Christian faith consciousness. In the Incarnation, God entered into time and space. These tangible basilicas built by Constantine could be seen and touched by pilgrims, and so they are a witness of the incarnational principle of the Christian faith. Seeing the holy places became a way of renewing the image of what had happened there in the life, ministry, death, resurrection, and Ascension of Jesus. Holy places begin to develop the notion of a "Holy Land" in the minds and hearts of Christian believers.

Jerusalem

By the end of the fourth century A.D., Christian pilgrimage to Jerusalem had become widespread. Pilgrimage to the Holy Land became a form of devotion and an enduring aspect of Christian piety. The late-fourth century pilgrimage account of Egeria, mentioned above, also records the devotional customs of pilgrims when they visited these sites. Scripture readings, prayers, hymns, antiphons, and the celebration of the Eucharist became parts of the ritual of Christian pilgrimage. That Christians could gather for worship at the very spot where the saving events had taken place made a lasting impression on pilgrims.

This devotional pilgrimage ritual gradually developed into stational liturgies, that is, rituals celebrated at the very spot or "station" of the saving event. These stational liturgies were another witness to the Christian sanctification of space. Stational liturgies incorporated ceremonial movement, solemn processions, and ritual expressions at the very site or between the sites of worship. As early as the late-fourth century, during the high liturgical celebrations of the year, Christian pilgrims could be seen in Jerusalem and other places in the Holy Land making their way through the streets as they sang hymns, chanted psalms, paused for prayer and listened to the Scriptures being read.

The early Christian pilgrims to the Holy Land developed a kind of tactile piety. Images and impressions were gained through touch, sight, and smell. Acts of pilgrimage devotion now became associated with holy objects like relics, bones, tombs, places, shrines, sacred texts, and liturgical vessels. This tactile piety is another form of an incarnational spirituality, a belief that God and the holy can be experienced through the senses, since God became incarnate in time and space. Early Christian pilgrims to the Holy Land bathed in the Jordan River where Jesus was baptized, kissed the relic of his true Cross, touched his tomb, and gathered oil pressed from the olives trees in the Garden of Gethsemane.

Bethlehem

Besides Jerusalem, the two other pilgrimage sites of importance were Bethlehem and Nazareth. Christian pilgrims wanted to see the places not only of Jesus' death, resurrection, and ascension, but also the places of his life. Bethlehem was the site of his birth (Matthew 2:1; Luke 2:4), and Constantine built a magnificent basilica over the spot where Christians venerated this event. The manger of Luke's gospel story (2:7) became identified as a cave near the town. The early theologians Justin Martyr and Origen identified this grotto as the site of Jesus' nativity. Earlier, in 135 A.D., the Roman Emperor Hadrian had constructed a sacred grove to Adonis over the place, ironically marking the spot in an attempt to paganize this site of Christian devotion. In this way Hadrian unwittingly assured that the Christians would remember the site. So, Constantine's workmen began construction of the Basilica of the Nativity at that place. Constantine even placed a jewel-covered crib in the crypt of the basilica as an object of devotion.

Bethlehem had an importance as early as the Old Testament. In Hebrew, the name of the place means, "house of bread." After the conquest of the land under Joshua, the place was settled by members of a clan from Ephratha (Joshua 15:59). Bethlehem is the setting of the love story between Ruth and Boaz as told in the book of Ruth. Other famous Bethlehemites included Jesse, and his son David, future king of Israel. Young David wandered the hills and fields around Bethlehem as a shepherd boy and later was anointed king of a new dynasty there by the prophet Samuel (1 Samuel 16:1–13).

After the fall of the Northern Kingdom of Israel to the Assyrians in 721 B.C., the prophet Micah (5:1–3) announced the future Messiah would be of the house of David and would be born in Bethlehem. Christian theology interprets this prophecy as being fulfilled in Jesus the Messiah and his Birth in Bethlehem. Matthew's gospel quotes it as part of the birth narrative (Matthew 2:6). Bethlehem became esteemed by Christian pilgrims as the actual spot of the Birth and Incarnation.

The name of the place, in Hebrew "house of bread," also became a point of meditation and theological reflection for the early Christians. "House of bread" took on a Eucharistic significance. Jesus, the bread of life (John 6:51), is born in the "house of bread." The name Bethlehem, in the Christian interpretation, points toward the fact that he will give his very flesh for the life of the world (John 6:54–58). Already in his birth, the sacrifice of Jesus for the salvation of the world is foreshadowed. The Eucharistic meaning of the nativity of Jesus is emphasized by the very name of the place where he is born.

Nazareth

Nazareth, as the scene of Jesus' childhood (Mark 1:9; Matthew 2:23; Luke 2:39) was almost equally important to the Christian pilgrims. Two of the earliest churches built there were over the sites of the home of Joseph (Matthew 1:18–25) and over the place where the Angel Gabriel visited Mary at the Annunciation (Luke 1:26–38). The basilica of the Annunciation was first constructed under the supervision of a certain deacon named Conon in the third century A.D. But this site had apparently been venerated by the early Christians decades before, as is attested by the pilgrim graffiti written to honor Mary and Jesus that has been uncovered by archeological excavations underneath Conon's basilica.

Nazareth is not mentioned in the Old Testament. The fact that Nazareth was not highly regarded may be evidenced by the remark of Nathaniel from Cana who asked: Can anything good come out of Nazareth? (John 1:46) It is referred to frequently, however, in the New Testament because of its connection to Jesus. It was the place of his conception (Luke 1:26–38), his childhood (Luke 2:39–40, 51–52), and the place of a key scene at the beginning of his public ministry when he lays down his program for his mission (Luke 4:16–30). It is also the place of a painful rejection of Jesus during the earthly ministry (Mark 6:1–6; Matthew 13:54–58).

Nazareth, as the site of the conception of Jesus, became associated with Mary and her role in salvation history in the minds of the early Christians. Joseph was also venerated there, but because of the lack of information about him in the New Testament after the childhood of Jesus, he is overshadowed by Mary, who lives to see the death and resurrection of Jesus. The New Testament provides more information about Mary during the public ministry of Jesus (Mark 3:31–35 and parallels) and ultimately through his execution (John 19:25–27), Resurrection, and the later event of Pentecost (Acts of the Apostles 1:14).

The Christian pilgrims wanted to see the very spot where the Angel Gabriel explained God's plan to Mary. The place where Mary uttered her "fiat," her *yes* to her role in God's plan to be the mother of the Messiah, drew them into reflecting on the awesome mystery of the Incarnation. Also, the humble life of Joseph, Mary, and Jesus in Nazareth was itself a teaching on the self-emptying of God who became poor so that the human race might become rich in grace and salvation. The so-called "hidden years" of the Holy Family in Nazareth became a source of a spirituality, which valued the sanctity of daily life and ordinary temporal affairs.

VISITING THE SACRED PLACES IN THE HOLY LAND

Jerusalem

Perhaps the best place to begin the visit to Jerusalem is the Mount of Olives. A splendid view of the city unfolds from here. The view which is afforded is the side of the Temple, whose site is indicated by a vast terrace and the gilded Dome of the Rock. According to Mark and Luke, this was the side of Jerusalem that Jesus himself gazed upon as he rode down the Mount of Olives on a donkey on Palm Sunday. At that time, the platform of the Temple was surrounded by colonnades and occupied by grandiose buildings. Mark and Luke state that Jesus entered the city through the gate that gave direct access to the Temple area (Mark 11:11; Luke 19:37,45). The gospel accounts of Jesus' triumphal entry into Jerusalem on Palm Sunday recall the prophecy of Zechariah, "On that day, his feet shall stand on the Mount of Olives, which lies before Jerusalem on the east . . ." (14:4–5).

81

Later tradition insists that the gate that Jesus rode through was the Golden Gate. This twin-arched gate, which is now bricked up, still preserves the elements of the Herodian construction, which existed at the time of Jesus. It is uncertain when the gate was bricked up, but the reasons for doing so were probably religious. The Golden Gate was perceived as too important for daily use. This gate was connected in the Christian imagination with a few key events in salvation history. Besides Jesus' use of it on Palm Sunday and Good Friday, it was also believed to be the site of Peter's healing of the lame man in Acts of the Apostles 3:1–10. According to popular early Christian tradition, it also was believed to be the site of the meeting of Joachim and Anne, after they had received the good news about the child that they would have by God's grace. Their child was Mary, the Mother of the Savior.

Golden Gate, Jerusalem
Courtesy of Biblical Archaeology Society

Interestingly, the three major religions that are present in Jerusalem even today have given the Golden Gate an important religious significance. In the Middle Ages, Jews would visit the site of the Golden Gate to pray, as they do today at the Western Wall. Christians became convinced that the Second Coming of Jesus at the end of time would occur at this site. "Behold, the Judge is standing before the gates" (James 5:9). For Moslems as well, this gate is the site of final judgment. For this reason there is a large Moslem cemetery in the Valley of Jehoshaphat, which is the place of the future judgment of the nations, according to the prophet Joel. "I will gather all the nations and bring them down to the valley of Jehoshaphat, and I will enter into judgment with them there . . ." (3:2). So, looking at Jerusalem from the Mount of Olives, the pilgrim gazes on the horizon of key events of salvation history, in expectation of the fullness of salvation at the end of time.

History

The Mount of Olives, which gives such a wonderful view of Jerusalem, is perhaps an appropriate place to give a brief overview of the most important dates in the complicated history of Jerusalem and the Holy Land.

Between the death and resurrection of Jesus in Jerusalem and the re-establishment of Christianity by Constantine in 313 A.D., Jerusalem and many sites of the Holy Land suffered from a few Jewish rebellions and Roman repressions. In 66 A.D., a Jewish Zealot rebellion erupted in Jerusalem, which spread throughout Judea and Galilee. This was during the reign of Emperor Nero. Nero sent Vespasian and his son Titus to suppress the Jewish revolt. Vespasian then became Emperor and Titus sacked Jerusalem in 70

A.D. All the survivors of the city were sold into slavery. The Temple was destroyed and the treasury of the Temple was brought back to Rome. Some of the Christian community managed to escape from the city.

This marked the end of Temple worship for Judaism. The leaders of the Jewish community then became the Rabbis. The next Jewish revolt against Roman oppression occurred during the reign of Emperor Hadrian in 132–134 A.D. This time the suppression was even crueler. More than half a million Jews were killed, and the Emperor razed 455 villages and desecrated many places of both Jewish and Christian worship. Hadrian transformed Jerusalem into a new city called *Aelia Capitolina*. He constructed a Temple to Jupiter over the site of the Tomb of Christ. A shrine dedicated to Venus was constructed over the site of Calvary, and the Cave of the Nativity of Jesus in Bethlehem became a shrine to Venus and Adonis. Jews were forbidden to enter into Aelia Capitolina except on one day of the year. This law was maintained until 313 A.D., when Constantine legalized Christianity.

According to Eusebius of Caesarea, Constantine built basilicas over the three so-called "mystical caves" of the Holy Land. The caves were the Cave of the Nativity in Bethlehem, the Cave of the Holy Sepulchre and Resurrection in Jerusalem, and the Cave on the Mount of Olives, at the site of the Ascension of Jesus. More Churches, shrines, and monasteries followed these basilicas. Under the successors of Constantine, the Holy Land became part of the Eastern Roman Empire known as Byzantium. More Churches and pilgrim hostels were built and Christian pilgrimage to the Holy Land flourished.

In 636 A.D., Syria and Palestine fell into the hands of Moslem Arabs. Jerusalem was occupied in 638 A.D. The Caliph Omar, kin to the Prophet Muhammad, came to visit Jerusalem, since it was considered holy by Moslems, due to its connection to Abraham. Moslems also believed that from Mount Moriah, which is in the Temple area, the Prophet Muhammad mystically ascended into Heaven. Christian and Jews were given certain freedoms under Moslem rule. At the end of the 7th century, the Dome of the Rock was built over the site of Mount Moriah on the platform of the former Jewish Temple. The plan of the Dome imitated the Rotunda of the Basilica of the Holy Sepulchre built by Constantine over the site of the Tomb of Christ. Jerusalem then became one of the three most important sites of Moslem pilgrimage. Christian pilgrims were still able to visit the Holy Land during this time.

Only in 1009 A.D., under the extremist Caliph al-Hakim, did the persecution of Jews and Christians begin. However, Moslems also had to face unreasonable restrictions under al-Hakim. He considered himself to be divine and was the founder of the Druze sect within Islam. It was al-Hakim who ordered the destruction of the Holy Sepulchre. The successor of al-Hakim, Caliph al-Zakir, gave permission to rebuild the Holy Sepulchre. The flow of pilgrims to the Holy Land was halted by invasions of the Seljuq Turks in 1070 A.D. This indirectly led to the first Crusade, proclaimed by Pope Urban II in 1095 A.D. Four years later, political order was re-established by Arabs in the Holy Land, but the Crusade had already begun. In July 1099 A.D., Jerusalem was taken by Geoffrey de Boullion, who proclaimed himself the baron and defender of the Holy Sepulchre.

Crusaders restored and rebuilt many of the shrines of Holy Land. However, the siege of Jerusalem and other cities in the Holy Land by the Crusaders led to the massacre of many of the Moslem inhabitants. This started a long-lasting animosity between Christians and Moslems. The Jews also suffered under the Crusaders' rule.

In 1187 A.D., a battle between the army of Saladin and the Crusader army at the Horns of Hattin ended in a victory for the Arabs. This was followed by one hundred years of wars. In 1291 A.D., the last Crusader fortress was taken by Bahri Mamluks, who were Turks introduced into Egypt by Saladin. The Mamluks had no respect for the Christian holy places and destroyed many of them. The rule of the Mamluks did not stop Christian pilgrimage to the Holy Land all together. But Palestine became a distant and relatively inaccessible province. The Ottoman Turkish conquest of this area changed little. Under the Ottoman rule, conflicts among Christian denominations over custodianship of various holy places developed. Not infrequently, Turkish Moslem supervisors were introduced to keep Christians from fighting over the shrines! This sad tradition of discord still persists and is manifested even today in the division of holy places into confessional areas where access is denied for liturgies of Christians of other denominations.

In the 19th century, Jewish refugees, fleeing persecution in Europe, began to settle in Palestine and Jordan. At the end of World War I, Palestine, Iraq, and what was known as the Transjordan was given by mandate to Britain by the League of Nations. Britain was supposed to prepare the Arabs and Jews for self-rule. But the rising of nationalism in both nations made this task impossible. Hitler's persecution of the Jews sped up the settling of Jews in Palestine and raised the question of a Jewish national state. The Arab desire for an independent state also intensified. Britain announced that the mandate for Palestine and the Transjordan would expire on May 14, 1948. That same day, the State of Israel was proclaimed by the Jewish leader Ben Gurion, and the first Jewish-Arab war began. In 1949, the armistice of Israel with Egypt, Lebanon, Jordan, and Syria was the impetus to the first large-scale displacement of Arabs from Palestine—the estimates vary from 600,000 to 800,000 displaced Arabs.

The wars of 1967 and 1973 between Israel, Jordan, Egypt, and Syria resulted in Israeli control of Jerusalem, the West Bank of Jordan, and the Gaza Strip. The political resolution of conflict between Palestinians and the Israeli State is still in the midst of a slow peace process. One of the biggest issues is the status of Jerusalem, which both Israelis and Palestinians consider their capital. Free access to the holy places of the city is still an unresolved issue. There are still difficulties for Christian, Jewish, and Moslem pilgrims in visiting sites which might be venerated by more than one faith.

The Mount of Olives

At the highest point of the Mount of Olives stands the Greek chapel of *Viri Galilaei*—"men of Galilee." Two columns in the Chapel mark the spot where two angels dressed in white addressed the Disciples after the

Ascension of Jesus. "Men of Galilee why are you standing there looking up at the sky? This Jesus . . . will return . . ." (Acts of the Apostles 1:11).

At the lower level of the slope of the Mount of Olives is a hermitage of Russian Nuns which includes the Church of Mary Magdalene, built in 1855 by the Russian Czar, Alexander III over the place where Orthodox Christians believe the Ascension to have taken place. The seven striking golden domes of the Church imitate the Russian architectural style of the 17th century. In the territory of the hermitage are remnants of a 6th century Armenian monastery. The Church houses the tomb of Grandducchess Elizabeth Fedorovna, who was murdered by the Communists in 1917. Of particular beauty are the view of Jerusalem and the panoramic of Judea from the hermitage, but the strict rule of the hermitage does not allow visitors.

Between the Chapel of Viri Galilaei and the Russian hermitage stands the Church of the *Pater Noster*—the "Our Father." This Church was built in the 19th century by French Carmelite Nuns. The Lord's Prayer is inscribed on the interior walls of the Church in a variety of languages. In the territory of the convent, excavations have revealed remnants of the large basilica built by Emperor Constantine in the 4th century. This was one of the three basilicas built over the "mystical caves" of the Holy Land. The Constantinian basilica was known as the Church of Eleona, from the Greek word *eliaon,* meaning "of olives."

About 100 yards up the hill from the Carmelite Pater Noster Church stands the Dome of the Ascension, called

Imbomon, from the Greek *in bommo,* "on the hill," and is venerated as the place of the Ascension. In 386 A.D., according to tradition, a shining Cross marked the spot. By 392 A.D., a beautiful Church, modeled on concentric circles, was built here. The present building, of Crusader construction, is a modest reminder of the ancient basilica. It occupies only part of the central circle of the original basilica. Beside this building is a small mosque, because Moslems also venerate memory of the Ascension of Jesus into Heaven.

Chapel of the Ascension,
Mt. of Olives, Jerusalem
Courtesy of Biblical Archaeology Society

Reflection

At this site, the pilgrim is invited to ponder the reality of the Ascension of Jesus. This event is not a "sad goodbye" or an "ending to the Jesus story." In many ways, it is a new beginning. The forty days of Resurrection appearances were a time of spiritual preparation for the Apostles, who would then take up the mission of Jesus, empowered by the Holy Spirit (Acts of the Apostles 1:4,5, 8). Ascension is the prerequisite for Pentecost and the age of the Church (John 16:4–7).

The Ascension is about the glorified state of being that Jesus has after the Resurrection. His exaltation attests to his sovereignty in the universe as he reigns as King of Kings and Lord of Lords at the right hand of the Father in Heaven (Mark 14:61–62). At the Father's right hand, Jesus is an advocate for the faithful (Romans 8:34). And as a result of the Ascension, the Holy Spirit can now be poured out in power upon the members of the Church (Ephesians 4:8–12). The challenge for the pilgrim is to recognize the presence of Jesus which now "fills all things" since the Ascension. The heights of the heavens and the depths of the abysses are charged with the presence of Christ. And the believer is called to give witness in hope to the future promise of glory symbolized by the Ascension.

As the Preface for the Eucharistic Prayer for the Ascension states, in part:

Christ, the Mediator between God and man, judge of the world and Lord of all, has passed beyond our sight, not to abandon us, but to be our hope. Christ is the beginning, the head of the Church; where he has gone, we hope to follow. . . .

The space between the Churches of the Mount of Olives is filled with many gravesites, ancient and modern. The presence of these burial sites reminds the pilgrims of the eschatological meaning of the Mount of Olives. It was here that the time of the Church began, after the Ascension in Acts of the Apostles 1–2. And it is here that the Lord will appear as judge at the end of time, according to tradition. Pilgrims standing in the interim time between the Ascension and the Second Coming of Jesus are

90

assured of the presence of Jesus by the promise of Matthew 28:20 "And behold, I am with you always, until the end of the world."

From the top of the Mount of Olives, the road leads down to Gethsemane and passes by the Franciscan Church of Dominus Flevit, "the Lord wept." This small Church was constructed in 1955 by the Italian architect Antonio Barluzzi on the site known as the place of Jesus' weeping over Jerusalem in Luke 19:41–44. Excavations during the construction of the Church revealed an ancient necropolis, used between 136 B.C. until 300 A.D. The tombs of Christians have engravings of crosses as well as monograms of Christ. Inscriptions on the ossuaries mention names common in the New Testament. In the 5th century, a Byzantine monastery existed here. The window over the altar offers an incomparable view of Jerusalem.

This panoramic view reminds the pilgrim of the humanity of Jesus who wept from compassion over the fate of Jerusalem and Israel, just as the prophet Jeremiah had done before the Exile. Jesus mourns over the

Panoramic of Jerusalem from the Church of Dominus Flevit, Mt. of Olives, Jerusalem
Courtesy of author, Dr. Irena Vaisvilaite

presence of sin and evil, which would lead to destruction. Each believer is also called to lament the presence of injustice, evil, and oppression in the world (Matthew 5:4).

 ## Gethsemane

The name of Gethsemane is derived from the Hebrew expression *Gat Shemen* which means "olive press," a reference to the natural abundance of olive trees and to the presence of oil presses in the region. Gethsemane holds an important place in the Gospel story, since Jesus spent the night before his arrest there, after eating the Last Supper with his Disciples (Mark 14:32–42; Luke 22:39–46; Matthew 26:36–46; John 18:1–11). The Mount of Olives was the way that Jesus used for his coming and going to Jerusalem. The mount was the way to an easy escape into the Judean desert, but he refused to use it even when his arrest became imminent. After the Last Supper, Jesus descended from the side of the city across the Kidron valley to the foot of the Mount of Olives, but did not go up the hill, towards escape. He stayed here, in the garden, where, the Gospels say, he used to come often.

Reflection

At this site the pilgrim is challenged to be united with the suffering and agony of Jesus, which is done by entering into one's own deepest pain, vulnerability, and suffering. Saying "yes" to the Father's will, in spite of great personal cost, is what the scene of the Agony of Jesus models. In Gethsemane, it is clear that Jesus was not a passive victim of circumstance. He gives himself freely, with full knowledge and determined purpose. The "cup" of the Passion is shared by every believer (Mark 10:38–39) who lives the pattern of the Paschal Mystery in daily life. Experiences of loneliness, fear, betrayal, darkness, and anxiety are opportunities to enter into this aspect of the Jesus story. The Garden setting, where salvation was once lost (Genesis 3:1–24), is now the site where redemption will be won (John 18:1; 19:41).

The exact spot where Jesus prayed in Agony before his arrest is unknown, but since early Christian times, this place has been venerated. The first shrine to this episode during the Passion of Jesus, when he made a free and conscious choice to do the Father's will, was perhaps in the 4th century, but destroyed in an earthquake in 745 A.D. The Crusaders built a shrine here in the 12th century. The Franciscans built the present Church, known as the Church of All Nations, in 1924. Antonio Barluzzi was the architect.

Church of All Nations,
Mt. of Olives, Jerusalem
Courtesy of Holy Views, Ltd

The name of the basilica commemorates the contributions made by many countries for its construction. It is also known as the Basilica of the Agony in reference to the agony, distress, and anxiety that Jesus suffered on the eve of his execution. The porch of the basilica faces the Kidron Valley. Corinthian columns flank the pillars of the façade and each cornice bears the statue of an evangelist.

The triangular area over the great portal is decorated by a mosaic of Christ giving his heart to an angel, symbolizing that he is the one mediator between God and humanity who gives himself in sacrifice. On Christ's left stand the sick and poor; on his right are the powerful and wise. He makes the prayers of all his own, according to Hebrews 5:7, which is quoted beneath the mosaic. "He offered up prayers and supplications with loud cries and tears . . . and he was heard because of his obedience." The artist of the mosaic was Giulio Bargellini.

The entrance into the basilica is a bronze door on which is depicted the tree of life springing from a cross and evolving into four volutes, each of which frames a symbol of one of the four evangelists. Panels beneath each symbol contain the respective Gospel texts telling of the Agony. The building is divided into three aisles by slim columns and gives the impression of being one large hall. In front of the high altar there is a large fragment of rock on which tradition says Jesus wept and prayed the night before his death. The rock is entirely surrounded by a crown of thorns in wrought iron.

The mosaic over the main altar by Pietro D'Achiardi represents the Agony of Jesus and his comfort by an angel.

Above, the hand of God is shown extending the crown of ultimate victory, and, in the middle, between Heaven and earth, an angel descends, bringing comfort from on high. The presence of the angel teaches the pilgrim that even in the most intense struggle and wrestling with God's will, spiritual strength and help are close at hand (Luke 22:43–44). The dark, intense colors of this modern image, as well as the images over the side altars, were meant by the artist to convey the idea of Jesus' Agony. To bring to mind the nighttime of the Agony, the architect used violet-colored glass everywhere. The somber blue of a star-studded sky is reproduced in the ceiling; the stars being surrounded by olive branches, reminiscent of Gethsemane itself.

Outside the basilica of the Agony is situated the Garden of Olives. Behind an iron fence, eight hoary olive trees are seen. There has been much discussion about their age. They are mentioned for the first time in the 15th century and, for pilgrims of subsequent ages, they impress as being very old and among the largest trees in Palestine.

Tomb of Mary and Grotto of Betrayal

Across from the basilica of Gethsemane, to the right, when facing the Kidron valley, is situated the Tomb of Mary and the Grotto of the Betrayal of Jesus. The Christian pilgrims of the 4th through the 6th centuries venerated the Agony of Jesus and his arrest in two different places. Pilgrims were accustomed to visit the Church of the Assumption, where the Virgin Mary's tomb was to be found, and then to continue on to the Grotto of the Betrayal, before going on to venerate the Agony of Jesus in the Garden. After this they would ascend the Mount of Olives. Today the entrance into the Grotto of Betrayal and into the Tomb of Mary is from the same courtyard, which is below ground level. When descending the stairs into the courtyard, on the right is a narrow corridor that leads into the Grotto of Betrayal. The arched door in the medieval façade leads to a long downward staircase to the Tomb of the Virgin.

The Grotto of Betrayal

Christian tradition associates this place with the meeting of Jesus with Judas after his Agony. In this same grotto of Gethsemane, various ancient documents cite the eating of a meal, in the course of which Jesus washed the feet of his disciples. There is mention of this meal in the writings of Archdeacon Theodosius and in the anonymous little work called "The Jerusalem Breviary." In ancient times, guides would

The Garden of Gethsemane, Mt. of Olives, Jerusalem
Courtesy of Biblical Archaeology Society

96

even show pilgrims the four (sometimes three) seats on which Jesus and his disciples sat. Out of devotion, pilgrims used to eat meals in the Grotto. Such meals, mentioned by tradition, could be based on the "suppers" of early Christians eaten at some of the holy sites associated with Jesus.

The Gethsemane supper is mentioned in a sermon attributed to Patriarch Eutychius of Constantinople in the 6th century, together with similar meals taken on Mount Zion and in Bethany. In the 4th century, the Grotto was transformed into a chapel. Remains of an altar have been found by archeologists, along with a kind of ambulatory shaped around it. Four pillars supported the roof of the chapel, which was lit by an opening in the roof. A small cistern was dug beneath this opening to hold rainwater. The Grotto was also used over the centuries as a Christian cemetery. Archeologists have discovered forty-two tombs under the soil which date from the 5th to 8th centuries, but the Crusaders also used this site as a burial place.

Various graffiti and decorations have been found from medieval times. The floor of the chapel was embellished with pieces of marble. The ceiling was decorated, mainly with star designs. According to the 12th-century pilgrim, John of Wurtzburg, the sanctuary was decorated with wall paintings, representing the prayer of Christ in the garden, Christ with the Apostles, and the Angel comforting Christ. Under these images, which have nearly all vanished by now, was an inscription that is still visible. "Here (in these representations) the King sweated blood. Christ the Savior frequented this place with his Apostles. My Father, if it is your wish, let this chalice pass from me."

Reflection

The Grotto of the Betrayal leads to a reflection on the "death he freely accepted" in order to defeat sin, evil, and the powers of darkness. Christ's death is a victory over the greatest enemy of the human race—death itself (1 Corinthians 15:25–26, 55). Therefore, when exiting the Grotto of the Betrayal, the next visit to the Tomb of the Virgin Mary enables the pilgrim to ponder the victory over death, which had its first fruits in the Mother of Jesus, who was taken into Heaven after her earthly sojourn.

The Tomb of Mary

The death and assumption of Mary into Heaven, proclaimed as dogma by Pope Pius XII in 1950, is described in an apocryphal writing called the "Transition (or "Dormition") of the Virgin." This text gives witness to the veneration of Mary's Tomb at the foot of the Mount of Olives since the 2nd century, when the site was transformed into a sanctuary.

History

The excavations of Mary's Tomb, carried out by the Franciscan Bellarmino Bagatti, showed that the surrounding Christian cemetery witnesses to the cult of this tomb. Mary's Tomb itself, originally made up of three chambers, was dug out with the same techniques used in tombs of the first century. The actual tomb was the inner chamber of the whole complex. These archeological findings, along with literary sources and liturgical devotion, witness

98

to the cult of the Tomb of Mary next to Gethsemane since the beginning of the Christian era. The first small Church built over the tomb was constructed around the beginning of the 5th century and consecrated by the Patriarch of Jerusalem Juvenal just after the Council of Chalcedon (451 A.D.). This Church was completely destroyed before the arrival of the Crusaders. The Crusaders rebuilt the Church about 1130 A.D. The upper Church was again destroyed by the Saladin after 1187 A.D. The Moslems respect the crypt today in veneration of the "Holy Mother of the Prophet Jesus."

The shrine was under the custody of the Franciscans from the middle of the 14th century until the 17th century, when it was taken back by the Greek Orthodox and Armenians. The Catholics are allowed to celebrate officially in the sanctuary three times a year, including August 15, the feast of the Assumption. The Syrians, the Copts, and the Abyssinians have minor rights.

Entering the Tomb

The actual façade of the building of Mary's Tomb is an austere and solemn Crusader construction. A long stairway leads down toward the Tomb. At the left is the Chapel of St. Joseph. The tombs on the sides of the stairway and next to the entrance of the tomb are of noble European Ladies related to the Crusaders who were the rulers of Jerusalem. Mary's Tomb itself is a small cell, which now has two openings for the movement of pilgrims. The rock, on which the body was believed to be laid, is protected by crystal, but nevertheless consumed by pilgrims who, for centuries, have been carrying away fragments of the stone. The opening in the ceiling has not only a functional purpose, but also a symbolic meaning. It indicates the opening of Heaven for Mary and for all believers, saved by the death and resurrection of Jesus.

Reflection

The shrine of Mary's Tomb invites the pilgrim to perceive the connection between Mary and her Son in the plan of redemption. The sword which barred access to the tree of life after the fall of Adam and Eve (Genesis 3:24), is now the sword which pierces the heart of Mary (Luke 2:34–35) in her role as the Sorrowful Mother at Calvary. At the foot of the tree of her Son's Cross, Mary became the "Mother of the Church," the new Eve beneath the "tree of Life" whose fruit is immortality (John 19:26–28). The Dormition or Assumption of Mary testifies to her "body and soul" sharing in this fruit of immortality.

As the Opening Prayers for the Solemnity of the Assumption of Mary state, in part:

> *All powerful and ever-living God, you raised the sinless Virgin Mary, mother of your Son, body and soul to the glory of heaven. May we see heaven as our final goal and come to share her glory.*

> *In the plan of your wisdom, she who bore the Christ in her womb was raised in glory to be with him in heaven. May we follow her example in reflecting your holiness and join in her hymn of endless life and praise.*

And as the Preface for the Eucharistic Prayer for the Solemnity of the Assumption states, in part:

Today the virgin Mother of God was taken up into heaven to be the beginning and pattern of the Church in its perfection, and a sign of hope and comfort for your people on their pilgrim way. You would not allow decay to touch her body, for she had given birth to your Son, the Lord of all life, in the glory of the incarnation.

The Assumption of Mary, then, is a type of "preview" for the Christian of the future glory that awaits every believer in the Resurrection on the last day. "For the trumpet will sound, the dead will be raised incorruptible, and we shall be changed" (1 Corinthians 15:52).

Mount Zion and the Upper Room

Any visitor to Jerusalem should not miss the Upper Room or Cenacle, situated on Mount Zion, outside the city walls. From the Tomb of Mary it is possible to reach there by the steep road called Derech Ha'ofel, which goes around the city walls and turns into another road, Ma'aleh Hashalom, passing the city of David and the Zion Gate. If proceeding from inside the city walls, it is necessary to pass through the Zion Gate. In front of the gate are the Benedictine Abbey and the Basilica of the Dormition. The basilica was completed by Kaiser Wilhelm II in 1910 and is believed to be built over the site where the Virgin Mary fell asleep for the last time. The architect, Heinrich Renard, used as a model the Carolingian Cathedral of Aix-la-Chapelle. Previously on this site was a Crusader Church of Our Lady of Mount Zion, which was demolished by Arabs in 1219 A.D.

Behind the Abbey is the small Franciscan Church of the Cenacle, built in 1936. The staircase outside of the Church leads to the Cenacle, the room of the Last Supper, located on the second floor. A tradition that reaches back to at least 348 A.D. states that here, in the southwest angle of the western hill of Jerusalem, is the site of the Last Supper, the Resurrection appearance, and the Descent of the Holy Spirit at Pentecost.

The Cenacle Room of the Last Supper, Jerusalem

Courtesy of Biblical Archaeology Society

Bishop Epiphanius (310–403 A.D.), a native of Palestine, basing himself on documents of the 2nd century writes: "Hadrian . . . found the city entirely razed to the ground and the Temple of God destroyed and trampled upon, with the exception of some houses and a certain small Church of the Christians, which had been constructed in that place, in which the disciples, after the Savior was taken up to heaven from the Mount of Olives, betaking themselves, mounted to the Cenacle."

The Cenacle, otherwise known as the "Upper Room," is a large hall. The ceiling is supported by pillars that divide the room into three naves. The pillars, arches, windows, and other gothic style architectural elements indicate a Crusader construction in the early 14th century. The Crusader structure was built over a much older structure, which, according to archeologists, was a Church-Synagogue of the early Christian community of Jerusalem.

Reflection

This place brings to the mind of the pilgrim the Biblical scenes of the institution of the Eucharist and the foot washing scene of the Last Supper (Mark 14:17–26; Luke 22:14–20; Matthew 26:26–30; John 13:1–20), as well as the Resurrection appearances (John 20:19–23), and the descent of the Holy Spirit at Pentecost (Acts of the Apostles 1:13; 2:1–4). These facets of the Christ mystery dynamic all intersect in this holy site. The pilgrim is challenged to enter into these scenes of salvation history by reflecting on the initiation sacraments of Baptism, Confirmation, and Eucharist, which plunge each believer into these aspects of the Paschal Mystery. The Cenacle enables the believer to appreciate how these sacraments are lived out on a daily basis. And from this "Upper Room" experience, the pilgrim is sent out on mission in the world to live the dying and rising of Jesus, empowered by the Holy Spirit and the sacramental life of the Church.

As the Preface for the Eucharistic Prayer of Pentecost states, in part:

Today you sent the Holy Spirit on those marked out to be your children by sharing the life of your only Son, and so you brought the paschal mystery to its completion. Today we celebrate the great beginning of your Church when the Holy Spirit made known to all peoples the one true God, and created from the many languages of man one voice to profess one faith.

Pentecost, the "birthday of the Church," is commemorated in the Chapel of the Descent of the Holy Spirit. The staircase to the left in the Upper Room leads to this chapel. There is a Moslem niche in the Cenacle indicating the direction of Mecca for Moslem prayers. Below the Cenacle is the room where King David's Tomb has been venerated by Jews and Christians since the 12th century.

Golgotha and the Basilica of Holy Sepulchre

The Death and Resurrection of Jesus took place outside of the city walls. Today this area is in the midst of urban construction. Over Golgotha and the site of the tomb, Constantine built a large and complex conglomeration of buildings. The present Basilica of the Holy Sepulchre takes up only a small, although central, area of this ancient territory.

History

Archeological excavations done during the 1961 restoration work ascertained that the area around the Garden of Golgotha served as a stone quarry between the 8th and 1st centuries B.C. When the quarry was abandoned in the 1st century B.C., the excavated area was transformed into a garden, resulting in a well-protected area outside the city walls of Jerusalem. Various tombs were dug into the high walls surrounding the Garden of Golgotha. Among these is the kokhim tomb, popularly known as the tomb of Joseph of Arimathea.

Archaeological evidence shows that the tomb of Jesus had been dug out in an isolated spur of the quarry. This new tomb facing east had a low door and was enclosed by a big slab. On entering the low opening, a vestibule was to be found, leading into the funerary chamber. Here only one funerary bench had been made in the northern wall. In this funerary chamber and on this funerary bench, the dead body of Jesus was laid. And it is from this tomb and from behind this "big stone" that victory over death was proclaimed through his Resurrection. Today the tomb is completely covered by marble slabs.

The Garden of Golgotha was enclosed inside the city wall by the third perimeter wall, which was completed by Agrippa I (41–44 A.D.). During this time the Christians of Jerusalem visited the site of the Garden of Golgotha and there celebrated the "Memory" of the great events of the crucifixion, death and resurrection of the Lord.

Due to the internal turmoil in the city, just prior to the first Jewish Revolt (66 A.D.) the members of the Mother Church fled the city to the town of Pella of the Decapolis, situated across the river in the northern part of the Jordan Valley. The First Jewish Revolt ended in a blood bath and the destruction by the

Roman Army of the magnificent Temple of Jerusalem. In its aftermath, the Judeo-Christians returned to the city to join the Gentile-Christians of the Mother Church who had remained here. But the situation in the city remained uncertain and very tense. The city was now guarded by the Tenth Legion, which put out the fire of revolt again in 116 A.D. and the final outbreak of violence in 133 A.D. This last outbreak is known as the Second Jewish Revolt led by Simon Bar Kochiba. These events also led to drastic changes in the architectural layout of the city.

Emperor Hadrian suppressed the revolt in 135 A.D. and decided to demolish the whole city of Jerusalem in order to erase all sites which could incite another revolt by the Jewish people. The emperor also forbade any Jewish presence in the new city. A Gentile-Christian community continued to live in Jerusalem and they ensured the continuity of identification of the sacred sites.

Hadrian prepared a completely new city structured on Hellenistic plans and renamed it "Aelia Capitolina" In this new architectural plan the Garden of Golgotha became the center of the new city. Hadrian built a pagan temple on the east-west axis of Golgotha. St. Jerome, in a letter to Paulinus in 395 A.D. says that:

"Since the times of Hadrian up to the empire of Constantine, for almost 180 years, the statue of Jupiter was venerated on the place of the Resurrection and on the rock of the cross a marble statue of Venus placed there by the Gentiles. In the intentions of the perpetrators of the persecutions they would have removed our faith in the resurrection in the cross had they profaned the holy sites with idols."

In the 4th century A.D., Constantine, in his intention to venerate the most sacred places of Jerusalem by building a basilica over the Holy Sepulchre and over the place of Resurrection, again changed the whole area. Here a building in the form of the royal Roman mausoleum was to be erected which was to become known as the *Anastasis* (Resurrection). The spur of Golgotha too was trimmed on the northern and western flanks to give way to the new construction, which was to leave Calvary outside of the new building.

The new building was comprised of five structures that covered the whole area previously occupied by the pagan temple of Hadrian. The *Martyrium* was a five-nave basilica, terminated by an apse and a raised presbytery where the main Sunday and festive liturgies were celebrated. Twelve silver columns surrounded the main altar on the presbytery.

Behind the apse of the basilica was a large cloister-garden that served to join the Martyrium with the Anastasis. This open air three portico cloister was "guarded" by the bare rock of the spur of Calvary left under the open sky in the southwest angle (adorned with precious stones and surmounted by a cross protected from the weather by a gilded ciborium). It is because of this bare rock of Calvary that the basilica was called Martyrium as the pilgrim Egeria recounts: "It is called the Martyrium because it is in Golgotha behind the Cross, where the Lord suffered."

Behind the cloister garden stood a circular Church, the Anastasis (Resurrection), with the Tomb of the Redeemer in the center. From the sources of the time and from the recent archaeological research carried out, it is possible to reconstruct the structure built over the tomb of the Redeemer: the façade had eight doors over which opened up eight windows elongated skywards. The rotunda was supported by twelve massive columns alternated by three groups of pillars that supported a balcony and over which rose a cupola with an "oculus" (eye). All around the lower part of the rotunda, large decorated windows filtered the light which filled this space. Light came in from the façade, from the windows and from the "oculus" because here the light of the Resurrection won over the powers of darkness. Constantine wanted the inner tomb itself to remain completely bare because no human decoration could embellish this site which witnessed the light of Resurrection. The exterior was richly decorated.

This beauty and richness vanished in 614 A.D. when the city of Jerusalem was conquered by the Persian hordes. The churches of Constantine on Calvary and of the Sepulchre were destroyed, as was most of the city. The damage was soon repaired by the monk Modest, who could perform the restoration, thanks to the generous help from the Christians of Tiberias, Damascus, Tyre and Alexandria. During this restoration, the spur of Calvary was covered up by a church.

The arrival of the Arab conquerors in 638 A.D. did not alter the status of this shrine. In the account by Eutichius, patriarch of Alexandria, it is said that a conqueror, Omar ibn al-Khattab, paid a visit to the Church of the Resurrection and sat in its courtyard. At the time of prayer, however, he left the Church and prayed outside, fearing that future generations might use his prayer inside the Church as a pretext for converting it into a mosque. Eutichius further says that Omar ibn al-Khattab also wrote a decree, which he handed to the Patriarch, in which he prohibited that Moslems gather in prayer at the site.

In later years, the basilica and the Anastasis suffered from earthquakes and fires. Each time, however, they were repaired through the great sacrifices of the Christian community of Jerusalem. In 1009 A.D., all of the buildings were again destroyed and the Holy Sepulchre was half-demolished by the will of Caliph al-Hakim. His successor gave permission to rebuild the Holy Sepulchre Basilica.

The Crusaders conquered Jerusalem on July 15, 1099. It was their intention to give back to the Holy Sepulchre its splendor. The Crusaders conceived the idea of uniting the scattered sanctuaries, found at the site at their time, under one new monument in the form of a cross. The Holy Sepulchre was repaired and an aedicula placed over it; the Rotunda was conserved in great part, furnished with a grand triumphal arch opening onto the new Church erected on the former garden, provided with a tribune and surrounded by an ambulatory. The arms of the transept could not be of equal proportion in order to retain in the northern one the portico of the garden known as the "Arches of the Virgin," and in the southern one the Chapel at Golgotha. To the east the new building had to be limited by the little oratories, in memory of certain events of the Passion, which opened onto the ambulatory. From the ambulatory also descended a stairway to the Chapel of St. Helen and the Crypt of the Finding of the Cross. A Romanesque façade was opened on a Southern courtyard where at its northwest corner a five-story belfry (48m) was built. At the northeast corner a separate monumental access to Calvary was built.

This new basilica, mainly preserved today, was consecrated on the 50th anniversary of the Crusader conquest of Jerusalem, as can be read in a Latin inscription engraved on the bronze main door: "This holy place has been sanctified by the blood of Christ, therefore our consecration adds nothing to its sanctity. However, the edifice which covers this holy place has been consecrated on the 15th of July by the Patriarch Fulcherius and by other dignitaries, the IVth year of his Patriarchate and the 50th anniversary of the capture of the city, which at the time shone as pure gold. It was the year 1149 of the Birth of Christ."

Jerusalem was reconquered by Arabs in 1188 A.D. The Church of the Holy Sepulchre was closed, and no one could officiate in it. In 1246 A.D., the keys of the basilica of Holy Sepulchre were given to two Moslem families who were to open the doors of the basilica to the pilgrims who arrived at the site. These "keepers of the keys" are still a reality today!

This was the time when various colonies coming from Mesopotamia, Egypt, Armenia, Ethiopia, Syria, Greece and Georgia established themselves all around the Holy Sepulchre. This is a very dark period in the history of this holy shrine. Unscrupulous public officials played games with the Christian willingness to get into this holy building and bring it back to life. Public auctions were held on multiple occasions. And the sanctuary gradually decayed.

The western powers, after failing several attempts to conquer the Holy Sites, tried to secure agreements that would ensure the worship at the site and assistance to the pilgrims. For the Western Christians, this right was given to the Franciscan Order. The papal Bull "Gratias Agimus" of Pope Clement VI, written to the general of the Order of Friars Minor, established that "the Friars of your Order may live permanently at the Church of the Sepulchre and there solemnly celebrate the Masses and the other divine offices." The Franciscans were in fact given the Chapel of the Apparition of the Risen Christ to his Mother, a place they have never left since.

The Russian Archimandritte Gretenius, who came in pilgrimage in the first years of the 15th century, says that within the basilica lived permanently a Greek priest, a Georgian, a Frank (that is a friar minor), an Armenian, a Jacobite and an Abyssinian (Ethiopian). This was a period of relative calm, when all the Christian denominations present at the Holy Sepulchre succeeded in finding a way to live together, and even celebrate Holy Week together, including the pilgrimage of Palm Sunday.

In 1500 A.D. and in 1700 A.D., Franciscans provided a reinforcement of the dome. In 1808 A.D., a large fire destroyed the Anastasis. This time reconstruction was provided by the Greek Orthodox community, and canceled all signs of Latin Christianity. In 1971 an agreement among the three communities gave the possibility of beginning a renewal of the dome over the Holy Sepulchre. It was completed in 1997.

Visiting the Holy Sepulchre

The Courtyard of the Basilica of the Holy Sepulchre is formed by the walls of the Crusader building and by the massive bell tower. To the right from the entrance is the Greek Orthodox monastery of Abraham, which is a recollection of the Christian tradition that this is the place of the sacrifice of Abraham.

The entrance has a double door, but one of them has been bricked up since the time of the Moslem reconquest of Jerusalem. The Basilica of the Holy Sepulchre is a rather complex building, which belongs to five Christian communities with different liturgies. Roman Catholic liturgy is celebrated daily by the Franciscans in the so-called Chapel of the Franks, located just to the right of the entrance. This chapel is dedicated to Our Lady of Sorrows and St. John. Tradition makes it the site where Mary withdrew, during the preparation for the Crucifixion. In the inferior floor of this chapel is a small space from which, in past centuries, poor pilgrims, who could not afford to pay the entrance fee to the Keyholders, could contemplate Calvary.

Today the Basilica is open daily and pilgrims can reach Calvary immediately from the hall of the basilica. A stairway on the right from the entrance takes pilgrims to the top of the hill. The mosaics on the ceiling were designed by P. D'Achiardi, who has preserved a medieval figure of Christ. The lateral mosaics, done by L. Trifoglio, represent "The Crucifixion," "The holy women at the foot of the Cross" and "The sacrifice of Isaac, symbol of Christ."

Tradition places the erection of the Cross and the Death of Jesus in the eastern part of the nave on the left, which belongs to the Greek Orthodox. A silver disk with a central hole, underneath the Greek Orthodox altar, marks the spot where the Cross stood. The site of the Crucifixion has been fixed since Constantine's time when at this site he had erected a wooden cross replaced in 417 A.D. by the Emperor Theodosius II with another cross made of gold and precious stones.

On each side of the Orthodox altar, a black marble disk recalls the memory of the two thieves crucified with Jesus, "one on the right, the other on the left" (Mark 15:27). To the right of the altar an opening in the pavement shows the cleft that tradition links to the earthquake mentioned in Matthew 27:51. The dominating figures in this central nave, besides the Crucified Lord, are the silver icons of the Virgin Mary and St. John who stood at the foot of the Cross (John 19:26–27).

The Basilica of the Holy Sepulchre, Calvary altar
Courtesy of Holy Views, Ltd

Coming down from Calvary, on the way to the Holy Sepulchre, in front of the main entrance of the Church, lies what has become known as the Stone of the Unction. In Jerusalem the scene of the taking down from the Cross was usually linked to that of the anointing. The spot of the Anointing of the corpse of Jesus has been venerated since the end of the 13th century. A stone covers the rock on which the body of Jesus would have rested. Early pilgrims described this stone as black, green or white. Today it consists of a red polished block.

Reflection

Venerating this site, the pilgrim is overwhelmed with the tangible, historical fact of the Death of Jesus. The central belief of Christians is that the crucified Jesus has been raised from the dead. The Cross was the key to the identity of Jesus as Messiah, and it is the key to the identity of any disciple of Jesus (Mark 8:31–37). Embracing the Cross fulfilled the mission of Jesus and characterizes the vocation of every Christian. The Crucified Christ is the wisdom of God and the power of God (1 Corinthians 1:18–25). As the Apostle Paul taught, what looks like foolishness, failure, and defeat in the eyes of the world, is actually wisdom, power, and victory in light of the Cross.

The Christian is one who has been crucified with Christ, so that the power of God can shine through in the life of faith (Galatians 2:19–20). It is precisely the paradox of the Cross which is the source of power, healing, forgiveness, and new life. Weakness, failure, and vulnerability can actually be the entry points for God's grace to penetrate the life of the believer. This is the paradox of Good Friday for Jesus and for every disciple (2 Corinthians 12:7–10).

As the Preface for the Eucharistic Prayer for Good Friday states, in part:

The suffering and death of your Son brought life to the whole world, moving our hearts to praise your glory. The power of the cross reveals your judgement on this world and the kingship of Christ crucified.

Here at the site of Calvary, life was restored through the wood of the Cross. The pilgrim is invited to a deeper participation in the new covenant sealed through the shed blood of the Lamb of God who takes away the sins of the world.

 ## Anastasis

After coming down from Calvary and passing by the Stone of the Unction, the pilgrim proceeds toward the Rotunda of the Anastasis (Resurrection) at the center of which lies a free-standing Aedicula. Here is a circular slab surmounted by an iron cage and the dominant supporting columns of the rotunda. The Aedicula is built completely out of marble slabs, which were placed there to cover the ruins which the tomb had become in 1009 A.D., when it was broken down by the will of the fanatic Caliph al-Hakim. The Aedicula comprises the outer Chapel of the Angel and the internal funeral chamber.

In the center of the Chapel of the Angel stands a marble base, which, according to tradition, contains the only remains of the boulder which once closed the entrance to the tomb. The actual sepulchral chamber is a small and awe-inspiring candlelit space. A marble slab protects the rock of the tomb. Over the

tomb, there are a great number of silver lamps, which belong to the three Christian denominations who share the property of the tomb: Catholic, Greek Orthodox and Armenian Orthodox. It is here that Christ completed his earthly mission before his glorious Resurrection in accordance with the prophecies. A small arched opening leads from the Chapel of the Angel to the funeral chamber. Since the destruction of 1009 A.D., only the lower parts of the chamber subsist, visible behind the icon, which is opposite the entrance and in the altar of the Copts, which backs onto the monument.

The Basilica of the Holy Sepulchre, Entrance to the Tomb of Jesus
Courtesy of Holy Views, Ltd

The recently renovated Dome of the Anastasis is the only visible expression of Resurrection symbolism. The state of the

116

Basilica cries aloud for restoration and even more—for the unity of Christians whose division is most visible and painfully apparent at this place.

Reflection

The Resurrection was the moment when death became life. Salvation, therefore, depends on this central event of salvation history (Romans 10:9). At this site, the pilgrim is invited to experience the interior spiritual power of the Resurrection in daily life (Philippians 3:7–11). This Resurrection offers each believer a new birth to a living hope in Jesus' victory (I Peter 1:3–8). The rising of Jesus is the promise of God's future for every believer. In the midst of suffering, absurdity, meaninglessness, hatred, or death, the believer can find, through faith in the Risen Lord, new meaning, new hope, and new life.

As the Preface for the Eucharistic Prayer for Easter states, in part:

In him a new age has dawned, the long reign of sin is ended, a broken world has been renewed, and man is once again made whole.

He has made us children of the light, rising to new and everlasting life. He has opened the gates of heaven to receive his faithful people. His death is our ransom from death; his resurrection is our rising to new life. The joy of the resurrection renews the whole world. . . .

Bethlehem

Bethlehem is a small town south of Jerusalem. The local population depends financially on tourism and produces beautiful crafts made from "mother of pearl" and olivewood. These crafts were actually introduced to the Holy Land by the Franciscans.

In the Bible, Bethlehem is called "Bethlehem of Judah" to distinguish it from the other Bethlehem which was in the north, in the territory of Zebulun. Bethlehem is first mentioned in the Bible in connection with the death of Rachel (Genesis 35:16–20). The story of Ruth, the Moabite, who accompanies her mother-in-law back home and meets Boaz in the fields, also took place here (Ruth 1:18–22). Bethlehem was also the birthplace of King David. When King Saul was rejected by God, Samuel went to Bethlehem where he anointed David as king of Israel (1 Samuel 16:4–13). But the "glory" of Bethlehem was yet to come. This was the town from which the "new David" was to come, as points the prophet Micah:

But you, Bethlehem Ephrathah, though you are small among the clans of Judah, out of you will come for me one who will be ruler over Israel, whose origins are from of old, from ancient times. Therefore Israel will be abandoned until the time when she who is in labor gives birth and the rest of his brothers return to join the Israelites. He will stand and shepherd his flock in the strength of the Lord, in the majesty of the name of the Lord his God. And they will live securely, for then his greatness will reach to the ends of the earth. And he will be their peace (Micah 5:2–5).

Site of the Nativity

The story of the birth of this "new David" is told by the Evangelist Luke. He states that the decree of Caesar Augustus, ordering a census of all the provinces subject to the Roman Empire, brought Mary and Joseph from Nazareth to their native city:

"In those days Caesar Augustus issued a decree that a census should be taken of the entire Roman world. (This was the first census that took place while Quirinius was governor of Syria.) And everyone went to his own town to register. So Joseph also went up from the town of Nazareth in Galilee to Judea, to Bethlehem the town of David, because he belonged to the house and line of David. He went there to register with Mary, who was pledged to be married to him, and was expecting a child. While they were there, the time came for the baby to be born, and she gave birth to her firstborn, a son. She wrapped him in cloths and placed him in a manger, because there was no room for them in the inn" (Luke 2:1–7).

Reflection

The message of the Angel proclaimed the good news of salvation to the shepherds of Bethlehem. "Do not be afraid; for behold, I proclaim to you good news of great joy that will be for all the people. For today in the city of David a savior has been born for you who is Messiah and Lord" (Luke 2:10). This good news or gospel message prompts the shepherds to go and see the baby who will be their Savior. Their reaction to the birth event is to glorify and praise God for all they had seen and heard. The shepherds are a symbol of all the members of the Jewish people who will recognize their Lord and Messiah in Jesus (Luke 2:20).

The Gospel of Matthew tells the story of the Magi travelling from the East. In a "house" at Bethlehem, they found "the child with Mary his mother" (2:1–12). These Magi give homage to the child and provide him with rich gifts of gold, frankincense, and myrrh, suitable for royalty. The Magi are symbolic of the Gentiles who will come to faith in Jesus as Lord. "He will save his people from their sins" (Matthew 1:21). The salvation that this baby comes to bring will be universal—Jews and Gentiles will together form the one people of God. However, the character of Herod and his slaughter of the innocents (Matthew 2:16–18) demonstrate the opposition that Jesus will face in his own life and mission. Bethlehem is not only the birthplace of Jesus; it is also the site of the earliest rejection and opposition of him. The shadow of his future Cross is cast even over the Manger.

The Gospels do not mention the birthplace of Jesus after the event itself, but the tradition, held by the local Christian community was very strong. Writing about 155–160 A.D., St. Justin Martyr, a native of Nablus, speaks about the location of the Nativity in Bethlehem as a generally accepted belief. There would have had to have been some places venerated by

Christians in the first century, since after the second Jewish revolt, Emperor Hadrian profaned the town with a precise political stratagem to eradicate all the places of worship of the Jewish nation (including the Judeo-Christian sites). In Bethlehem he planted a sacred garden dedicated to Adonis on the holy grotto of the Nativity.

St. Jerome, in 396 A.D., wrote: "From Hadrian's time until the reign of Constantine, for about 180 years . . . Bethlehem, now ours, and the earth's most sacred spot . . . was overshadowed by a grove of Thammuz, which is Adonis, and in the cave where the infant Messiah once cried, the paramour of Venus was bewailed."

In the year 325 A.D., the Bishop of Jerusalem, St. Macarius, at the Ecumenical Council at Nicea, took the opportunity and asked the Emperor Constantine to repair the neglected holy places in his diocese. The Emperor ordered the construction of monumental churches to commemorate the three principal events of Jesus' life. One of these was to be a basilica of the Nativity.

Constantinian Basilica of the Nativity

The magnificent building built by Constantine had two atriums and five naves. An L-shaped stairway led from the Basilica to the Holy Grotto. The Grotto was transformed and the venerated manger was replaced by one of precious metal. St. Jerome complained that "we, as if this was to honor Christ, have removed the one made of clay and have substituted it with a silver one; but for me the removed one was more precious."

This basilica, constructed under the supervision of the Emperor's mother, St. Helen, survived until the first destruction occurred during the Samaritan revolt in 529 A.D. Damaged during this uprising, the Basilica was restored and embellished by

Basilica of the Nativity, Bethlehem
Courtesy of Biblical Archaeology Society

Emperor Justinian. The main modification to the Constantinian Church plan was performed at the "sacred area" above the grotto. It is at this time that the two side entrances were opened. It is also at this time that the whole grotto was vaulted in stone and an altar on the eastern side was built, under which the "exact birth-site of Jesus" started to be venerated. Justinian's building survived and today is still standing at the site of the Nativity.

St. Jerome in Bethlehem

Bethlehem was an important center of early Christian monasticism. In 382 A.D. from Rome, came Paula, a descendent of the old Roman aristocracy, with her daughter Eustochium and St. Jerome. Paula founded two monasteries, one for herself and her nuns, another for St. Jerome and his monks. Here Jerome wrote produced his Latin translation from the original Hebrew of the Old Testament, now known as the Vulgate.

Under Islam

With the occupation of Palestine by the Arabs a gradual decline of the Christian presence began. The Caliph Omar visited Bethlehem and promised that the Moslems would pray in the Church as individuals only, without assembly or muezzin. At Christmastime members of both religions performed their devotions together in the Church and, on the whole, lived on peaceful terms due to the common respect of Moslems and Christians for the birthplace of Jesus.

Crusaders in Bethlehem

The Crusader army under Geoffrey de Bouillon that arrived in 1099 A.D. regarded the Church of the Nativity as something peculiarly their own. On Christmas Day, 1100 A.D., Baldwin, the first king of the Latin Kingdom, was crowned in Bethlehem. His successor Baldwin II followed his example in 1122 A.D.

The Crusaders built next to the Basilica of the Nativity a cloister and monastery which was given to the Canons of St. Augustine. During the Latin occupation of Jerusalem

(1099–1187 A.D.), Bethlehem grew rich from the flow of pilgrims. It was decided that the Basilica should be properly restored. The Frankish kingdom and the Byzantine Empire helped the project, which was carried out between 1166 A.D. and 1169 A.D. The restoration affected most of the Church's interior.

Later centuries

With the end of the Crusader experience, Bethlehem passed definitively under Moslem rule but, notwithstanding the difficulties encountered, it remained for long centuries the principle Christian enclave of the Holy Land. In 1333 A.D., the Franciscans established themselves in Bethlehem in the deserted Augustinian monastery, where they still reside today. By 1347 A.D., the Franciscans were the custodians of the Basilica.

With the 16th century, the period of conflict between the Franciscans and the Greeks for the possession of the Sanctuary began. Consequently, the Basilica passed alternatively from the Franciscans to the Greeks according to the favor enjoyed at the Sublime Porte. During the war between the Ottoman Empire and the Republic of Venice (1646–1669 A.D.) which ended with the expulsion of the Venetians from the Island of Crete, the Greeks were authorized to take over the Grotto of the Nativity.

The population of Bethlehem today is made up of Christians and Moslems. Among the Christians there are Catholics of Latin, Syrian, Melchite, Armenian and Maronite rites. Orthodox Christians include Greek, Syrian and Armenian. Protestants are also present.

Visiting the Basilica of the Nativity

The square in the front of the Basilica was once a colonnaded atrium. The façade, now almost covered with later buttresses, once had three doorways. The only one remaining was reduced a few times. The interior of the Basilica includes five naves. Four rows of rosy columns divide the space. The interior, which is now darkened, was richly decorated during the Crusader restoration in the 12th century. Some of this decoration still remains. The best preserved decoration is the gilt mosaic and mother of pearl in the upper part of the central nave.

12th century A.D. gilt mosaic above columns central nave of Basilica of Nativity

Courtesy of author Dr. Irena Vaisviliaite

In the space between the windows is a procession of angels, all moving toward the East, as if going to adore the infant Jesus in the Holy Grotto. Under the windows, in very elaborate architectural compositions, were the scenes of the Ecumenical Councils of the Church and inscriptions, citing in Greek and Latin, the principal decisions of the main ecumenical and provincial councils of the Church.

The northern and southern frieze above the cedar wood architrave contained portraits of the ancestors of Jesus. The northern frieze depicted the genealogy of Matthew 1:1–16 while the southern frieze depicted that of Luke 3:23–38. Of these medallions only the first eight on the northern frieze have survived.

The rosy columns of the central nave, made from the red stone of Bethlehem, were depictions of Saints from East and

Interior of Basilica of Nativity, Bethlehem

Courtesy of Biblical Archaeology Society

West. These included St. Saba, St. Theodosius, St. George and Western Saints such as St. Cathaldus of Taranto. Eastern Saints depicted include St. Macarius, St. Euthimius, St. Canutos of Denmark, and St. Olaph of Norway. Most columns depict a single saint, although some have two. This is the most impressive collection of the Crusader paintings. Almost every pillar has graffiti below the painting, which is a testimony of pilgrims of different ages. Through the openings in the floor the remains of the original mosaic floor of Constantine's basilica might be seen.

The Cave of the Nativity

The Cave of Nativity can be entered from both transepts of the Basilica. The place of the Nativity is in the small apse containing the Greek Orthodox altar, used also by the Armenians. Under the altar is a silver star, inscribed: "Hic De Virgine Maria Jesus Christus Natus est, 1717," which means, "Here Jesus Christ was born from the Virgin Mary, 1717." In the dome of the apse is a mosaic of the Nativity, which depicts the Virgin reclining on her bed as she looks at the Infant. Beyond this are the ox, the ass, and the shepherds. The Latin inscription reads "Pax hominibus" (Peace to men).

The Manger

On the south side of the cave is the Grotto of the Manger. Although St. Jerome, as quoted above, complained about the original manger that was taken away, it is very possible that the manger still does exist under the present covering of marble slabs. The altar of the Adoration of Magi is Roman Catholic. The Franciscans daily celebrate the Eucharist of the Nativity here and at noon perform a procession around the Holy Places.

Reflection

The pilgrim to Bethlehem, in Hebrew, "House of Bread," is challenged to reflect upon the birth of Jesus as a "Eucharistic event"—the Word became flesh (John 1:14). Jesus, the "Bread of Life," is born in the "House of Bread," and he will give his very

The Cave of the Nativity, Bethlehem
Courtesy of Biblical Archaeology Society

flesh for the life of the world (John 6:51–58). The Incarnation foreshadows his becoming enfleshed in the sacrament of the Eucharist. The Eucharist is the food for the spiritual journey of the pilgrim. As the Preface for the Eucharistic Prayer of Holy Thursday states, in part: "As we eat his body which he gave for us, we grow in strength. As we drink his blood which he poured out for us, we are washed clean."

Bethlehem represents the astounding truth of the Incarnation, that the Creator becomes a creature. God becomes human; the supernatural enters into the natural. God enters into the messy and chaotic "stable of humanity." This involves a "marvelous exchange"—God became human so that humans might become God-like. This means that the ordinary human affairs of daily life can take on a whole new significance. Through the power of the Holy Spirit, daily affairs, actions, and duties can be occasions for God "taking flesh." God's glory can now be manifested in things human. Bethlehem challenges the pilgrim to consider how Jesus can be born into the joys and sorrows, hopes and fears, triumphs and disappointments of daily life.

As the Preface for the Eucharistic Prayer for Christmas states, in part:

> *Today in him a new light has dawned upon the world: God has become one with man, and man has become one again with God. Your eternal Word has taken upon himself our human weakness, giving our mortal nature immortal value.*

Nazareth

"It is because of Nazareth that Christ is called the Nazarene and from which, we who today are called Christians, were called Nazarenes" (Eusebius of Caesarea, early 4th century A.D.).

History

Nazareth was unmentioned in the Bible before the Gospel account. The Gospels state that Jesus' family came back here from Egypt (Matthew 2:23). Nazareth was the hometown of Jesus, where he had relatives (Matthew 13:54–56). Here Jesus went to the Synagogue to study the Torah and the Prophets, and to praise the Father. Here he worked with his own hands as a carpenter. From here he went to Jerusalem every year on the Jewish feasts of pilgrimage. And it is from here that he went to the Judean desert to start his public ministry and proclaim the "Good News" (Mark 1:9). Here Jesus returned during his public ministry and was rejected as a prophet when the townspeople wanted to throw him over the cliff (Luke 4:14–30). Afterward, Jesus left his hometown never again to set foot there.

But, after his death and resurrection, a Christian community arose in Nazareth. The Lord's "brethren" (Acts of the Apostles 1:14; 1 Corinthians 9:5) had a prominent place in the primitive Palestinian Church. James, the Lord's "brother," was a leader of the Church in Jerusalem (Acts of the Apostles 21:18). During the persecution in Asia Minor of Emperor Decius (249–251 A.D.), a Christian martyr, Conon, was brought to trial and he proclaimed in judgement: "I am from Nazareth of Galilee, I am a descendent of Christ to whom I give worship since my forefathers."

The Apocryphal writings, too, expand this vision about the next-of-kin of the Lord. They gather the oral traditions of the first Church about Jesus' family, especially his childhood years, and Mary and Joseph's daily life with Jesus among them. Thanks to this witness, the tradition of places, related to the life of Mary, Joseph and Jesus, was passed on. Pilgrimage to these sites started in the very early centuries of Christianity. At the end of the 4th century, two noble Roman women, Paula and her daughter Eustochium, came in pilgrimage to Nazareth, accompanied by St. Jerome. This indicates that Nazareth was already a pilgrimage site.

Archeological excavations have unearthed a Judeo-Christian structure over the house of Mary, which was the site of the Annunciation. Excavations also revealed a primitive baptismal font. This confirms a Christian presence in the town as well as veneration of the holy places since 1st century A.D. In the 5th century, a Church was built to substitute the previous structure over Mary's house, site of the Annunciation. The Church had

130

three aisles and a porch or atrium. This building remained in use from the 6th to the 12th centuries, though it was damaged and repaired several times. It disappeared only when the

Panoramic view of Nazareth

Courtesy of Holy Views, Ltd

Crusaders replaced it with another structure, just as it, in turn, had displaced the earlier Judeo-Christian structure.

The arrival of the Crusaders meant an era of splendor for Nazareth. The Crusaders rebuilt a magnificent Church in the Roman style with three naves, of which from the northern one it was possible to descend to a small grotto in which was venerated the record of the Annunciation and the sojourn of the Holy Family. Nazareth became also a bishopric seat. After the defeat of the Crusaders on July 4, 1187, Nazareth was taken, its population killed or imprisoned, and the sanctuary "renowned in the entire world" was profaned. In 1263 A.D., the magnificent Church of the Crusaders was systematically destroyed. Nazareth became a ghost town and only adventurous pilgrims succeeded to arrive at the site. These pilgrims give testimony of the existence of a small chapel to protect the Annunciation grotto "in memory to the humility and poverty." For four hundred years, nothing changed at this site.

In 1620, the Franciscans acquired the site. A community was installed there to keep guard over the venerable ruins. In 1730, the Friars were permitted to build a Church over the Grotto. This small building was built in the style of a martyria, allowing the faithful to see the Grotto under the altar. It was completely reconstructed in 1955, when the modern Basilica of the Annunciation was begun, built by an Italian architect, Giovanni Muzio. At the same time, a complete archaeological examination of the site and the building of a monument were conducted.

Today Nazareth, the political and administrative capital of Galilee, is a busy town with a population made up of Christians and Moslems. On the outskirts of the historic town, "new Nazareth," known as "Nazareth Elite," has grown. The dome of the Basilica dominates the skyline of the town over the site of the Annunciation.

Visiting the Basilica of the Annunciation

In the front of the Basilica is a large elevated square. A statue of the Redeemer crowns the façade of the Basilica. Below is a representation of the Annunciation and of the four Evangelists. Two doors open into the Church proper while, in line with these, there is a small eight-sided shrine, which is the baptistery. The great elevated square also serves another purpose:

132

to protect the remains of ancient Nazareth's dwellings, which have been excavated in the soil below. A portico graces the building on the western and southern sides. On the south side it forms a graceful open arcade overlooking the valley of Nazareth.

The Basilica consists of two levels, the Upper Church and the Lower Church, which are interconnected. The entrances to the Church are from the portico on the west side, in line with the whole building, and from the south in the direction of the Grotto. The side entrances in the main facade give access to two spiral stairways leading to the lower and upper Church.

The lower Church preserves the Holy Grotto and the remains of the Byzantine and Crusader Churches. The present Church almost exactly follows the plan of the Crusader basilica. The middle of this Church enshrines the most sacred spot of all, the Grotto of Annunciation, and here the roof of the lower Church is pierced by a star-shaped oculus situated exactly under the dome of the upper Church. The whole space is centered on the Holy Grotto. In the lower Church, visitors can also see the remains of an early Christian baptistery and the mosaic floor, inscribed "Gift of Conon, deacon of Jerusalem." The altar is from the 17th century, and bears an inscription: *Verbum Caro hic factum est:* "Here the Word became flesh" (John 1:14).

The Gospel of Luke records the encounter of Mary with the Angel Gabriel:

In the sixth month, the angel Gabriel was sent by God to a town in Galilee called Nazareth, to a virgin betrothed to a man named Joseph, of the house of David. The virgin's name was Mary. The angel went to her and said, "Hail, you who are highly favored! The Lord is with you." Mary was greatly troubled at his words and wondered what kind of greeting this might be. But the angel said to her, "Do not be afraid, Mary, you have found favor with God. You will be with child and give birth to a son, and you are to give him the name Jesus. He will be great and will be called the Son of the Most High. The Lord God will give him the throne of his father David, and he will reign over the house of Jacob forever; his kingdom will never end." "How will this be," Mary asked the angel, "since I am a virgin?" The angel answered, "The Holy Spirit will come upon you, and the power of the Most High will overshadow you. So the holy one to be born will be called the Son of God. Even Elizabeth your relative is going to have a child in her old age, and she who was said to be barren is in her sixth month. For nothing is impossible with God." "I am the Lord's servant," Mary answered. "May it be to me as you have said." Then the angel left her (Luke 1:26–38).

The Upper Church can be accessed by stairs. This Church is the Latin Catholic Parish Church of Nazareth. Its doors, windows, walls and lantern are richly decorated. The mosaic behind the central altar is dedicated to the teaching of the Second Vatican Council and especially to the one, holy, Catholic and apostolic Church, which came to life through the Incarnation, Death, and Resurrection of Jesus. The striking dome, erected above the Grotto of the Annunciation, celebrates the event of the Incarnation and is designed to express a mystical numerical symbolism. The walls of the basilica are decorated with mosaic images of the most venerated Marian places of different countries. Overhead it is crowned by a row of windows, which throw impressive light on the main altar and apse.

From the square in the front of Basilica, the Excavations and Museum can be reached. Part of it can be viewed through a grill, but visitors also are admitted inside if accompanied by a curator. While excavating the area around the Annunciation site, the Franciscan archaeologists not only cleared the different monuments that were built on top of the shrine, but also had the privilege to examine attentively the uninterrupted veneration that Christians have treasured jealously through the centuries. These excavations, in fact, not only revealed the sanctity of the site, but also the remains of the ancient village of Nazareth with its silos, cisterns and other cave-dwellings.

The remains found under the Byzantine construction led the Franciscan archaeologists to conclude that prior to this period the Christians had already constructed a place of worship at this site. This grotto, known as that of Deacon Conon (from the name inscribed in a mosaic found here), yielded not only some graffiti on the walls but also decorated plaster. The graffiti bears witness to Christian devotion pre-dating the Crusaders.

Architectural elements and decorations suppose the construction of a "public" building, which the archaeologists identify with a church-synagogue. Among these architectural remains the archaeologists found various graffiti. Scratched on the base of a column appeared the Greek characters XE MAPIA, translated as: "Hail Mary." This inscription is the oldest known of its kind. It was written before the Council of Ephesus in 431 A.D., when devotion to Mary received its first universal impulse. Other graffiti, conserved at the museum, confirm the Marian nature of the shrine. One in Armenian reads "beautiful girl" (referred to Mary) and another one in Greek reads "on the holy site of Mary I have written."

In the museum is a set of beautiful capitals, fashioned to adorn the Crusaders' basilica. The capitals, however, were never set in place. They were rediscovered in all of their original freshness and beauty, perfectly preserved. The capitals represent various saints and the Virgin Mary.

Reflection

Nazareth plunges the pilgrim into the mystery of human obedience to the will of God. Mary's fiat is a challenge to every Christian who seeks to hear the Word of God and do it. Her "yes" to God's plan for her life was uttered in the midst of unknowing and uncertainty. During his earthly ministry, Jesus blessed his Mother, not for her physical motherhood, but rather for her obedience to God's word and her discipleship: "While he was speaking, a woman from the crowd called out and said to him, 'Blessed is the womb that carried you and the breasts at which you nursed.' He replied, 'Rather, blessed are those who hear the word of God and observe it'" (Luke 11:27–28).

The role of Mary in the plan of salvation shows how God exalts the humble and lifts up the lowly. Her vocation shows how

God has the power to reverse things—fruitfulness in virginity. Mary, a virgin, bears a child, God becomes human, and creation is renewed.

As the Opening Prayer for the Solemnity of the Annunciation states, in part:

> *Almighty Father of our Lord Jesus Christ, you have revealed the beauty of your power by exalting the lowly virgin of Nazareth and making her the mother of our Savior. May the prayers of this woman bring Jesus to the waiting world and fill the void of incompletion with the presence of her child.*

The figure of Joseph at Nazareth also invites the pilgrim to ponder trust and obedience to God's plan. Joseph is the just man who, through obedience to a dream revelation, takes Mary as his wife in a very

Basilica of Annunciation, Nazareth
Courtesy of Biblical Archaeology Society

compromising situation. Joseph receives his own "Annunciation" from an angel who calms his fears. "Joseph, son of David, do not be afraid to take Mary your wife into your home. For it is through the Holy Spirit that this child has been conceived in her. She will bear a son, and you are to name him Jesus . . ." (Matthew 1:20–21). Like his namesake in Genesis, Joseph receives a series of dreams which outline for him God's slowly unfolding plan for the Holy Family. Interestingly, Joseph never speaks a word in the Gospels, and yet his hidden, humble witness of fidelity, courage, and righteousness speaks louder than words.

As the Preface for the Eucharistic Prayer for the Feast of St. Joseph states, in part:

> *He is that just man, that wise and loyal servant, whom you placed at the head of your family. With a husband's love he cherished Mary, the virgin Mother of God. With fatherly care he watched over Jesus Christ your Son, conceived by the power of the Holy Spirit.*

The "hidden years" of the Holy Family at Nazareth are a pattern of spirituality which sanctifies the ordinary temporal affairs of family life. The Christian family is the "domestic Church," where the first lessons of the faith are learned and lived. Family relationships can be the primary context for growing in age, wisdom, and strength, as Jesus did in Nazareth with Joseph and Mary (Luke 2:51–52).

Spirituality of the Christian Pilgrimage to the Holy Land

For the Christian, the pilgrimage to the Holy Land is not simply an exercise in nostalgia, but it is an encounter with the Lord himself. The goal of the journey is to meet Jesus. Past events of salvation history are recalled and actualized at the sites where they took place in a kind of anamnesis experience, a rich, spiritual way of entering into the past event. Pilgrims do not indulgence in reminiscences; it is the relevance to their present existence of what happened in salvation history, and the capacity of these salvation events to nourish their spirituality that are important. The goal of the Holy Land pilgrimage, as with any Christian pilgrimage, is to meet the Lord and to be changed by becoming more like him. Pilgrimage devotion is more than just mere tourist curiosity. Contact with the sites of the Holy Land is a means of connecting with the events remembered in those locations for the purposes of personal spiritual growth and renewal. The story of the life, ministry, death, and resurrection of Jesus can be told and recounted in many places all over the world, but no verbal testimony can ever replace the witness of the actual places themselves. Because of the Incarnation, Christian memory is inescapably bound to place.

In this spirituality, Jerusalem itself becomes a symbol of salvation. This is true not only for Christians, but as mentioned above, it was true for the ancient Israelites. During the Exile, the city of Jerusalem lay in ruins, its Temple destroyed. But the prophets looked forward to a new city, a heavenly Jerusalem that became a symbol of salvation and deliverance. The exilic prophet Ezekiel portrays Jerusalem as an idyllic sacred city that is at the center of the world: "Thus says the Lord God: This is Jerusalem! In the midst of the nations I placed her, surrounded by foreign countries" (5:5).

Jerusalem, for Ezekiel, is a cosmic mountain, a juncture between heaven and earth, a focal point, an axis mundi, and a source of life, fruitfulness, healing, peace, and perfection (40:1–2; 47:1–12). However, Isaiah, of all the prophets, seems to contain the richest spirituality of Jerusalem. The end of the Exile, for example, is portrayed as the restoration of the city.

"Comfort, give comfort to my people, says your God. Speak tenderly to Jerusalem and proclaim to her that her service is at an end, her guilt is expiated" (40:1–2). "Yes, the Lord shall comfort Zion and have pity on all her ruins; Her deserts he shall make like Eden, her wasteland like the garden of the Lord; Joy and gladness shall be found in her, thanksgiving and the sound of song" (51:3).

The Psalms also provide a spirituality of Jerusalem. There is a subgrouping of Psalms known as the Psalms of ascent, used specifically by Jewish pilgrims as they ascended the Temple mount in Jerusalem. Psalm 122 reads, in part:

"I rejoiced because they said to me 'We will go up to the house of the Lord.' And now we have set foot within your gates, O Jerusalem—Jerusalem built as a city with compact unity. To it the tribes go up, the tribes of the Lord" (1–4).

Psalm 131 proclaims:

Zion is my resting place forever; in her will I dwell, for I prefer her. I will bless her with abundant provision, her poor I will fill with bread. Her priests I will clothe with salvation, and her faithful ones shall shout merrily for joy (131:14–17).

The New Testament picks up on this spirituality of Jerusalem and deepens it to a paschal significance. Jerusalem is the place of salvation because of the death and resurrection of Jesus. Jerusalem is the mother of Christians (Galatians 4:26) and it is the name that each Christian bears (Revelation 3:12). The builder and architect of this city is God (Hebrews 11:10), and its citizenship is gained simply through faith in Jesus (Hebrews 12:22–24, 28; 13:14). "You have drawn near to Mount Zion and the city of the living God, the heavenly Jerusalem, to myriads of angels in festal gathering, to the assembly of the first born enrolled in heaven . . ." (Hebrews 12:22–23).

Of all the New Testament books, Revelation presents the most profound theology of Jerusalem for the Christian pilgrim to the Holy Land. Jerusalem becomes an eschatological symbol, a salvific sign of future glory. The heavenly Jerusalem is called by God to be the city-Bride, the redeemed community of the Lord, risen and transformed, whose twelve gates bear the names of the twelve tribes of Israel, and whose walls are founded on the twelve foundation stones of the Apostles (21:1–4, 9–14). "I saw no temple in the city. The Lord, God the Almighty, is its temple—he and the Lamb. The city had no need of sun or moon, for the glory of the Lord gave it light, and its lamp was the Lamb" (21:22–24).

This eschatological symbol of Jerusalem became part of the liturgical theology of the Church. In its liturgy, the Church includes the theology of Jerusalem in its worship, ritual, prayers, and readings. For example, on the Feast of All Saints, November 1, the Preface for the Eucharistic Prayer states, in part:

"Today we keep the festival of your holy city, the heavenly Jerusalem, our mother. Around your throne the saints, our brothers and sisters, sing your praise forever. Their glory fills us with joy, and their communion with us in your Church gives us inspiration and strength, as we hasten on our pilgrimage of faith, eager to meet them. . . ."

The prayers, readings, and antiphons of the Rite of Dedication of a Church include several references to this spirituality of Jerusalem. For example, when the foundation stone for a new Church is laid, the bishop prays:

Lord, you built a holy Church, founded upon the apostles with Jesus Christ as its cornerstone. Grant that your people, gathered in your name, may fear and love you and grow as the temple of your glory. May they always follow you, until, with you at their head, they arrive at last in your heavenly city. We ask this through Christ our Lord.

When the site of a new Church is blessed, the antiphon that is sung is: "The walls of Jerusalem will be made of precious stones, and its towers built with gems, alleluia." Part of the Rite of the Dedication of the Church is to anoint the new building. This ritual includes twelve anointings inside the Church to signify that the Church is an image of the holy city of Jerusalem. After the litany of saints in the Rite, the bishop prays a long prayer of dedication of the Church, which states in part:

Father in heaven, source of holiness and true purpose, it is right that we praise and glorify your name. For today we come before you, to dedicate to your lasting service this house of prayer, this temple of worship, this home in which we are nourished by your word and your sacraments. Here is reflected the mystery of the Church. . . . The Church is favored, the dwelling place of God on earth: a temple built of living stones, founded on the apostles with Jesus Christ its cornerstone. The Church is exalted, a city set on a mountain: a beacon to the whole world, bright with the glory of the Lamb, and echoing the prayers of her saints. . . .

When the festive lighting of the altar and the Church takes place during the Rite, the antiphon sung is: "Your light will come, Jerusalem; upon you the glory of the Lord will dawn and all nations will walk in your light, alleluia."

The Preface to the Eucharistic Prayer in the Rite of Dedication of a Church reads, in part:

Father, all-powerful and ever-living God, we do well always and everywhere to give you thanks. The whole world is your temple, shaped to resound with your name. Yet you also allow us to dedicate to your service places designated for your worship . . . Here is foreshadowed the mystery of your true temple; this church is the image on earth of your heavenly city . . . You continue to build your Church with chosen stones, enlivened by the Spirit, and cemented together by love. In that holy city you will be all in all for endless ages, and Christ will be its light forever. . . .

143

Conclusion

In conclusion, how can a connection be made between the Jubilee 2000 and its inclusion of the Holy Land pilgrimage as part of its celebration, and this spirituality of Jerusalem? Interestingly, a link can be made through the holy door, the porta santa in Rome, which is a symbol of the holy year observance. The solemn opening of the holy door by the Pope at St. Peter's basilica in Rome marks the beginning of the Jubilee 2000. This ritual symbolizes entry into the house of God. Jesus is the door of salvation and eternal life. On another level, the human race is challenged to open wide the doors of their hearts to God. But what does the holy door symbolism have to do with Jerusalem?

The holy door at St. Peter's basilica in Rome was called the "golden door" or the "Golden Gate" in the Middle Ages. According to medieval piety, this door contained pieces of the Golden Gate, transported from the city of Jerusalem. As mentioned above, the Golden Gate was believed to be the one that Jesus passed through on Palm Sunday during his triumphal entry into the city. It was also believed that Jesus passed through this gate on Good Friday, carrying his cross, on his way to Golgotha. And the popular Christian apocryphal account of the immaculate conception of the Virgin Mary included the detail that her parents, Joachim and Anne, met and embraced at the Golden Gate of Jerusalem after they received the oracle that Mary was to be born.

Prior to 1500 A.D., Christian pilgrims to the Holy Land attest that one of the gates of Jerusalem was sealed up and only opened on two special occasions. On Palm Sunday and on the feast of the Exaltation of the Cross, the Golden Gate was opened up so that a solemn liturgical procession with the bishop could pass through it, to commemorate the sacred events. And pieces of the bricks which walled up the Golden Gate were considered to be precious relics for the medieval pilgrim.

The connection with the holy door at St. Peter's and the Golden Gate of ancient Jerusalem was an easy one to make in the creative imagination of medieval Christians. But the symbolism is still profound for the modern Christian pilgrim. The Jubilee is a celebration of redemption and the holy door tradition is a tangible sign of crossing the threshold of faith and of the millenium. To open the gates of heaven and eternal life, Jesus first had to pass through the Golden Gate of Jerusalem, symbolizing his suffering and death. And, so, too, Christians are challenged to enter into the fullness of salvation by passing through the holy door of the Jubilee, which symbolizes repentance, reconciliation, and conversion. "Happy are they who . . . have free access to the tree of life and enter the city through its gates. . . . The Spirit and the Bride say, Come!" (Revelation 22:14, 17)

FOUR

THE PILGRIMAGE TO ROME

City of Apostles, Martyrs, and Saints

Rome is the eternal city. Perhaps no other city in the world has played such an important role in the development of western civilization. All roads lead to Rome, as the familiar adage attests. During the height of its ancient Empire, Rome was the *caput mundi,* the head of the world. The lasting influence of Rome has impacted history, language, culture, politics, religion, and the fine arts of the western world.

The pilgrimage to Rome has been at the very heart of the Jubilee celebrations since the very first Holy Year in 1300 A.D. As mentioned in Chapter One, it was the occasion of the Christmas season "Veronica procession" in Rome, known as the "Jubilee," that prompted Pope Boniface VIII to proclaim the first holy year celebration in 1300 A.D. Pilgrimage to the city of the Apostles

147

Peter and Paul became the foundation upon which all other Jubilee traditions were based.

Since the second century A.D., Christian pilgrims have made their way to Rome to visit the "trophies" of the Apostles, the tombs of St. Peter and St. Paul. As the history of the Church unfolded, Rome became the city of Apostles, Martyrs, and Saints. And pilgrimage to Rome became an important element of Christian devotion. Rome became the "New Jerusalem" of the Christian world, a center of apostolic teaching, tradition, and spirituality. The Jubilee pilgrimage to Rome, initiated in 1300, institutionalized a long-standing Christian tradition of journeying to the tombs of the Apostles Peter and Paul in order to venerate the two "founders" of the "New Jerusalem." Indeed, the Jubilee indulgence could only be obtained by a pilgrimage *ad limina apostolorum,* literally to the "threshold of the Apostles," that is, the tombs of St. Peter and St. Paul.

The celebration of the Jubilee 2000, although extended to the Holy Land and the local churches, will have its center in the city of Rome. Literally millions of pilgrims will journey to Rome to visit the holy sites and participate in the Jubilee devotions, which have marked the Holy Years since 1300. Among the highlights of the Jubilee events in Rome will be the Eucharistic Congress.

. . . since Christ is the only way to the Father, in order to highlight his living and saving presence in the church and the world the International Eucharistic Congress will take place in Rome on the occasion of the Great Jubilee. The year 2000 will be intensely eucharistic: in the sacrament of the

148

Eucharist the savior, who took flesh in Mary's womb 20 centuries ago, continues to offer himself to humanity as the source of divine life (TMA 55).

 ## Christianity and the City of Rome

In the New Testament, the book of the Acts of the Apostles records the spread of the gospel by the Apostles. On the day of the Ascension, Jesus instructed his followers to be his witnesses in "Jerusalem, Judea, Samaria, and to the ends of the earth" (Acts of the Apostles 1:8). The geographical schema of the book of Acts begins in Jerusalem and ends in the city of Rome. In the closing chapters of Acts of the Apostles, the apostle Paul arrives in Rome under house arrest. And the final verses, Acts of the Apostles 28:30-31, describe St. Paul's ministry in Rome despite the conditions of being a political prisoner.

How is this geographical schema for the spread of Christianity in Acts of the Apostles 1:8 significant? What is the implicit view of the Roman Empire in Acts? It seems that the Apostles saw the Empire, which controlled most of the known western world at this time, as an instrument for the spread of the gospel. That is, they saw that under God's plan, his providence, the Roman Empire, with its common language, transportation, communication, travel, and commerce, was actually an excellent setup for their missionary efforts. The book of Acts of the Apostles sees the structure and context of the Roman Empire as being advantageous for the spread of the gospel. Acts of the Apostles sees the political structure or entity of the Roman Empire as part of God's plan for the missionary activity of the apostles.

149

There seem to be three basic reasons why the gospel spread so rapidly in the first century Roman Empire. First, the favorable material conditions of the Hellenistic culture were important. Having the same language, travel, commerce, common roads, etc., definitely aided the spread of Christianity. Secondly, the Empire provided favorable political and social conditions, since the world was at peace. There were no major wars going on at the time, because of the so-called *pax romana*, which is attributed to the Emperor Octavian Augustus. This period of peace also helped the movements of the Apostles and early Christian missionaries around the Mediterranean basin. And thirdly, the Empire provided favorable spiritual conditions. The first century Romans were abandoning their faith in the worship of the old pagan gods and goddesses. Certainly, publicly, the official Roman religion, the worship of the Roman gods, was adhered to, but privately, many were abandoning the state religion. Christianity met this need and satisfied this spiritual hunger.

Roman Forum, Rome, Italy
Courtesy of author Dr. Irena Vaisvilaite

150

When St. Paul arrives in Italy, and finally Rome, in the last few chapters of Acts of the Apostles, he finds a Christian community already present. There were already Christians in the city of Rome before St. Peter and St. Paul arrived. When did Christianity come to Rome, then? It seems that Christianity came very early to Rome, probably in the 40s. If the death and resurrection of Jesus occurred approximately in 33 A.D., this means that probably within ten years, the message of the Christian gospel had spread to the capital of the Empire already.

Two ancient Roman historians, Suetonius and Tacitus, testify to the existence of Christians in Rome in the 40s. Suetonius was a Roman historian who wrote about 115 A.D. He wrote a biography of the Emperor Claudius, who ruled in first century Rome during the 40s. In his *Life of Claudius,* Suetonius states that the Emperor Claudius "expelled the Jews from Rome because of their constant disturbances caused by Chrestus." Scholars have traced this to the expulsion of Christians from Rome in 49 A.D. The name Chrestus in Suetonius' book refers to Christ. Emperor Claudius expelled certain Jews from Rome who were causing disturbances because of Chrestus, Christ.

It seems that the early Christians were still part of the Jewish community, and they were causing disturbances by preaching about Christ, and so the Emperor Claudius expelled them from the city of Rome. There is evidence of this edict of Claudius even within the New Testament itself. In Acts of the Apostles 18:2-3, two Roman Christians, Aquila and Priscilla, are described as living in the city of Corinth because they were expelled from Rome by the edict of Claudius. The conclusion that can be drawn is that there were definitely Christians in Rome by 49 A.D., as this edict of the emperor Claudius demonstrates.

The second Roman historian who provides evidence of Christians in Rome in the 40's A.D. is Tacitus. Tacitus wrote about 112-115 A.D., and among his books is a work on the history of Rome called the *Annals*. In the Annals, Tacitus talks about the Emperor Nero who ruled in Rome in the 60's A.D. Tacitus tells the story of the great fire in Rome in 64A A.D., during Nero's reign. He recounts that Nero needed a scapegoat for the destructive fire, and so he blamed the Christians. A persecution of Christians then broke out; many were rounded up, arrested, tortured, and executed. So, Tacitus affirms that already by 64 A.D., the Christians are an identifiable group in Rome, they are no longer confused with the Jews. In fact, Tacitus says that large numbers of Christians were condemned, meaning that there was a large Christian community in Rome by 64 A.D.

The conclusion that can be drawn from Suetonius and Tacitus is that Christianity existed in Rome from at least the 40s, the time of Claudius' edict of expulsion. And by the 60s, the Christians were a large group, and were distinguished from the Jews, as is evidenced by the action of Nero to blame the Christians for the fire of Rome in 64 A.D.

Peter and Paul in Rome

The Apostles Peter and Paul do not seem to have arrived in Rome until maybe 60 A.D., so they were not the ones to bring the gospel to Rome first.

There were Christians already in Rome when they arrived. The Christian mission had spread to Rome from Jerusalem through others before St. Peter and St. Paul got there, as Suetonius and Tacitus make clear.

St. Paul seems to have arrived in Rome as a political prisoner about 60 A.D. St. Peter's arrival in the capital of the Empire is not recorded in the book of the Acts of the Apostles. In fact, the New Testament is silent about St. Peter's time in Rome and his eventual death there. But scholars posit that St. Peter arrived in the early 60s. If the New Testament itself does not provide information about the careers of St. Peter and St. Paul in Rome, then what are the sources for this information? Scholars appeal to the writings of early Christian authors from the 2nd century onwards. There are several sources from early Church fathers, or patristics, early Christian authors and theologians, who testify to the presence and martyrdoms of St. Peter and St. Paul in Rome.

In about the year 96 A.D., in a letter written by a certain Clement, bishop of Rome, there is evidence of the Apostles' presence in Rome. In I Clement, chapter 5, there is mention of St. Peter and St. Paul both being in Rome and dying as martyrs during the persecution of Nero between 65-67 A.D. The second historical source of the presence of St. Peter and St. Paul in Rome is from Ignatius, a 2nd-century bishop of the ancient city of Antioch. Ignatius wrote a letter to the Christians of Rome around 120 A.D. In it, Ignatius reminds them that St. Peter and St. Paul were in charge of the Church in Rome. In chapter four of his letter, Ignatius refers to St. Peter and St. Paul giving orders to the Church at Rome, that is, having spiritual authority. Therefore, Ignatius gives testimony of the Apostles being in Rome.

After the year 150 A.D. or so, there are many references to the presence of St. Peter and St. Paul in Rome, as well as their martyrdom. Early Christian patristics such as Irenaeus, Tertullian, Clement of Alexandria, and Origen, all make reference to the careers and executions of St. Peter and St. Paul in Rome.

 ## Martyrdoms of Peter and Paul

The emperor Nero succeeded Claudius as emperor of Rome and ruled from 54-68 A.D. It was during his reign that the first formal persecution by the Romans broke out against the Christians. And from 65-313 A.D., there were many persecutions against the Church, sometimes restricted to one area of the empire; sometimes they were Empire-wide persecutions. In fact, the early Church of the first few centuries is often called the "Church of the Martyrs," because there were so many people executed for their Christian faith.

The terrible fire in Rome and its aftermath prompted Nero's persecution of the Christians. In July of 64 A.D., a tremendous fire broke out while Nero was away; he was not even in the city. There seems to be evidence that Nero perhaps had the fire started himself because he wanted to create a new city. This fire raged for over a week and was by far the worst fire in the history of Rome. Of the fourteen regions into which the city was divided at that time, only four remained whole. Nero needed a scapegoat,

154

and so he blamed the fire on the Christians, as Tacitus recounts. It is this fire of 64 A.D. that is intimately linked with the martyrdoms of St. Peter and St. Paul. This fire was the determining factor for the Neronian persecution.

It is important to note that Nero was not persecuting the Christians for any philosophical, religious, or political reasons. He simply needed a scapegoat. Later on in the Empire, other emperors would persecute and execute Christians for religious or political reasons, but this was not the case during this first persecution. The Neronian persecution was confined to Rome and was not because of any ideological tension between the Church and the State. Nero just needed to blame someone for this fire in order to placate the crowds of Rome. So, Nero turned their anger and frustration on the Christians.

Nero organized huge public spectacles of torture in an area known as Nero's Circus, a large stadium used for chariot races and sports competitions that stood outside the walls of the city, in an area known as Vatican Hill. Today St. Peter's basilica stands on the site of this bloody episode in Roman history. In Tacitus' Annals, it is recorded that Nero had Christians wrapped in animal skins and eaten alive by beasts. He burned people at the stake, and had human torches to illuminate the stadium in the evening. Nero also had many Christians crucified in this Circus. Tacitus states that the tortures and executions were so cruel, that eventually people began to feel sorry for the Christians. Tacitus says: "the condemned were pitied . . . because they were sacrificed not for the common good, but because of the sadism of one individual. . . ."

155

The first wave of arrests seems to have been in 65 A.D., and it lasted until at least 67 A.D. During these years there were waves of persecution, it was not a daily occurrence. St. Peter and St. Paul were killed during this Neronian persecution. There are several ancient sources which say that the year of their martyrdom is 67 A.D. Nero himself was not even in Rome at this time. He went to Greece in 66 A.D. and remained there until 68 A.D. But he did not need to be present in order for his judicial decisions to be carried out. St. Peter and St. Paul are the two most famous victims of Nero's persecution. St. Peter was crucified in the Vatican circus, and St. Paul was beheaded outside the city on the road leading to Ostia. Many ancient Christian authors testify to the manner and place of the executions of the Apostles. Eusebius, a Christian historian who wrote the first history of the Church in about 325 A.D., says that St. Peter was crucified and St. Paul was beheaded during the reign of Nero. And, he says, their graves are in the Vatican garden and the Ostian way, respectively.

In the beginning of the 3rd century, in the 200s, there is quotation from a Roman Church official, Gaius, which says: "I can show you the trophies of the apostles. You will find their remains in the Vatican or along the road to Ostia. There are the trophies of those who founded this Church." This affirms that the graves of the Apostles were already being venerated or honored as sacred sites. These "trophies" are the memorials to the Apostles, the shrines, placed over their graves by the early Christian community to honor them and mark the spot. This means that the tradition of the trophies or memorial of the Apostles existed before 200 A.D., since Gaius makes reference to them.

The deaths of St. Peter and St. Paul in Rome made the city the spiritual capital of the early Church. The combination of the apostolic deposit of the teaching of St. Peter and St. Paul and the witness of their martyrdoms gave Rome a spiritual primacy among the other early Christian communities. As the early Christian writer Tertullian stated: "The apostles poured forth their whole teaching, along with their blood, into the Church at Rome." In this light, the martyrdoms of St. Peter and St. Paul take on a very deep spiritual and theological significance. The spiritual foundation of Rome as the "New Jerusalem," the spiritual center of Christianity, is the joint martyrdoms of St. Peter and St. Paul. St. Peter and St. Paul are the "founders" of the Church at Rome, not because they were the first ones to preach the Christian gospel there. Rather, their foundation is their witness of teaching and martyrdom, which forms the apostolic deposit, entrusted to the Church at Rome.

 ## Church of the Martyrs

The persecution under the Emperor Nero was only the first of many persecutions against the Christians in the Roman Empire. St. Peter and St. Paul were the two most famous victims of the Neronian persecution in the middle of the first century. But there were many other Christian martyrs in the first few centuries of the Church. From 65 A.D. until 313 A.D., and the Edict of Constantine, thousands of Christians made the ultimate sacrifice through their profession of faith in Jesus. The word martyr comes from the Greek word *martus,* which means witness. A martyr is a witness for Jesus. In the very act of dying for the true faith, the martyr gives witness to Christ.

A brief overview of the periods of persecution can be sketched after Nero up until the time of Emperor Constantine. As seen above, the Neronian persecution was not really ideological. Nero simply needed a scapegoat for the fire of 64 A.D. It was not until the Emperor Septimius Severus (193-211 A.D.) that an ideological persecution against the Christians was waged. Severus issued an edict, which forced Roman provincial governors to persecute Christians. Powerful written protests against the cruelty of this persecution were written by the Christian theologian Tertullian. This persecution died down with the new Emperor Alexander. Alexander was tolerant of Christianity. But with the assassination of Alexander, Maximin came to the throne in 235 A.D. and again stirred up anger against the Christian community. The next great widespread persecution came during the reign of Emperor Decius in 249-251 A.D.

Decius thought the Christians were a terrible poison in the Empire, since they did not engage in the official state religion and worship the old Roman gods. When Christians were arrested, they were forced to make public homage to the pagan gods. When they did not, they were tortured and killed. Many important Church leaders suffered heroically and died at the hands of their torturers, for example, the bishop of Rome, Pope Fabian died after torture.

The most severe of the periods of persecution came during the reign of Diocletian in 303-312 A.D. In 303 A.D.,

Diocletian ordered that all known public places of Christian worship be destroyed and their sacred books be handed over. Christians were forbidden to assemble and were to be denied the protection of the laws. A second more severe decree was issued by Diocletian, which singled out bishops, priests, and deacons for special attention. While later, great numbers of Christians from every rank were seized.

These horrendous persecutions, arrests, tortures, and executions did not end until Constantine became emperor and legalized Christianity with his Edict of Milan in 313 A.D. This was an incredible change from the decades of persecution, fear, and secrecy. Suddenly the Roman Emperor imposed restrictions on pagan religious practices and displayed Christian symbols publicly. Constantine attached the standards of the army to a Cross emblazoned with the monogram of Christ, and he even struck coins with a picture of himself wearing a helmet with this monogram of Christ on it. The monogram was of the two Greek letters chi (X) and rho (P), the first two letters of the name of Christ. This symbol of the P drawn over the X became a sign for Christ. Constantine increasingly identified the interests of the State with those of the Church, in seeking a unity of Church and State. Constantine's conversion was, without doubt, one of the greatest turning points in the history of the Church and in the history of western civilization.

At first, it seems puzzling that the Roman Empire considered Christianity such a menace and a danger. After all, Rome was tolerant in principle and allowed many religions to flourish. The Empire only declared "war" on the Christians when it realized that the aim of Christianity was the total triumph over all other religions. The Christian Gospel proclaimed the reality of the one true God. So, the Christian position was the absolute rejection of the worship of the old pagan gods and goddesses of Rome. This issue was an obviously religious one. But politically, the Roman authorities had problems with Christians also. Christians took a relative view of the civil authority of the Emperor and the Empire. According to the Christians, these civil authorities were only to be obeyed when they were in harmony with the will of the one true God, whose will had been revealed to his Church. This criterion of civil obedience was a threat to the Roman authorities.

Christians were thought to be disturbers of public order for basically two reasons. First, they did not participate in public ceremonies and thereby upset the gods. And secondly, they did not make ritual offerings to the cult of the Emperor in demonstration of their loyalty and obedience. Many Roman emperors were actually worshipped as demigods. For example, Domitian, 81-96 A.D., styled himself as "master and god." But the Christians would not engage in emperor worship, and therefore they were considered public enemies.

Theology of Martyrdom

During the decades of the period known as the "Church of the Martyrs," a theology of martyrdom developed. As mentioned above, the word martyr comes from the Greek word *martus,* which means witness. In the very act of dying for the true faith, the martyr gives witness to

160

Christ. Jesus told the Apostles on the day of ascension, in Acts of the Apostles 1:8 "You will be my witnesses in Jerusalem, Judea, Samaria, and to the ends of the earth." Through word and deed, the Apostles were to witness to the Gospel of Jesus to the ends of the earth. On a deeper reading of this verse, the word witness, or martures, can be interpreted as an allusion to the death that most of the Apostles would suffer for the sake of this Gospel. Christian tradition holds that the only apostle who did not suffer martyrdom was John. The Apostles, indeed all of the heroes of integrity who gave their lives for Jesus, were uniquely united with their crucified Master.

In the mentality of the early Christians, the concept of witness was linked with sacrificial dying. The experience of martyrdom was the ultimate participation in the Paschal Mystery, the dying and rising of Christ himself. The martyrs were seen as heroes, victors, who won the crown of victory from the Lord by their endurance and faithfulness to him. Just as star athletes in the ancient world won crowns of laurels in the Roman sports competitions, so too, did the martyrs win a spiritual competition with the powers of evil. They had won the palm of victory, and the crown of eternal life (Revelation 7:9-17). The martyrs have a place of honor in heaven, gathered around the throne of God.

Around the year 195 A.D., Tertullian wrote that "the blood of the martyrs is the seed of the faith." He believed that the blood shed by the martyrs acted as a seed for the faith of the Church. There was a saying in the East during Decius' persecution that for every one Christian killed, two more people embraced the faith of Christ. The faith, perseverance, and the heroism of the martyrs were a witness for the faith of the Church. By the example of the blood shed by these men and women, people were moved and inspired to embrace this faith that they were dying for. Devotion to the martyrs grew, and they were honored after their death. As early as the 200s, the private commemorations of the martyrs began to pass into the official and public liturgy of the Church.

The date on which a martyr died was considered his or her "birthday," *(dies natalis)* because they were born into eternal life. These anniversaries or "birthdays" of the martyrs were carefully remembered and so came to create the earliest Church calendars of feasts. For example, by 200 A.D., the Christians in the city of Rome celebrated the memory of St. Peter and St. Paul on June 29. And by the 300s, the relics or bones of the martyrs were placed under the altars in Christian basilicas. Martyrs were believed to have special powers of intercession for those Christians still on earth. It became a teaching of the early Church that the martyrs prayed for those still alive. The liturgies that were celebrated at the shrines, which were built at the tombs of martyrs, expressed the faith of the Church that, by dying for the faith, the martyrs had transcended into the realm of God. And there was believed to be a special presence of the martyr at his or her grave.

Besides the special presence of the martyr at the grave, it was also believed that there was a special presence of the martyr in the community which worshiped at the grave. This is the reason for the prayers, liturgies, and celebrations, which took place at the tombs of the saints and martyrs in the early centuries of the Church, and which continue today. In the early Christian mentality, the tomb of the saint or martyr became the meeting place between heaven and earth, a sort of "Jacob's Ladder"

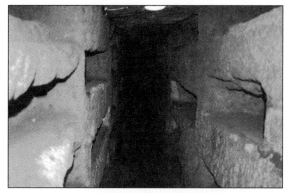

Interior of Catacombs of St. Sebastian, Rome, Italy

Courtesy of author, Dr. Irena Vaisvilaite

(Genesis 28:17), where God's eternal kingdom was made manifest in the here and now.

The powerful spiritual presence of the martyrs at their tombs was the reason for the development of the idea of Christian pilgrimage. A Christian pilgrimage is always made to a sacred or holy site—the tomb of a saint or martyr, or some place associated with that saint or martyr. Rome became a center for pilgrimage because of the many relics of saints and martyrs there.

Christian Pilgrimage to Rome

The graffiti in the catacombs, the inscriptions, and the frescoes all witness to a steady stream of pilgrims to Rome. And of course, the main focus of Christian pilgrimage in Rome was the tombs of St. Peter and St. Paul. It seems that the annual highpoint for pilgrimage was the feast day of St. Peter and St. Paul on June 29.

It became a custom in the early Church to visit the threshold of the Apostles, the *ad limina apostolorum,* to venerate the tombs of St. Peter and St. Paul. The fact that the tombs of the Apostles were the destination for the early Christian pilgrims can be confirmed by the above-mentioned words of the Roman cleric Gaius, in the 2nd century, "I can show you the trophies of the Apostles, if you will go as far as the Vatican or the Ostian way, you will find the monuments of those who founded this Church."

With the edict of Constantine in 313 A.D. legalizing Christianity, and the construction of the basilicas of St. Peter and St. Paul over the tombs of the Apostles, a new impetus was given to devotional visits to the Eternal City. Other churches that were built at this time were: Holy Cross basilica, St. Agnes, St. Lawrence, and St. John Lateran's basilica. Also at this time of the 4th century, the catacombs were decorated and inscribed with signposts and markers to help pilgrims find their way around. Pope Damasus, who was bishop of Rome in 366-384 A.D., began the proper care of the catacombs for sites of pilgrimage.

Rome was the place where many martyrs met their death in the early Church, and Christians wanted to come and venerate the tombs of the martyrs. The martyrs were considered to be powerful intercessors in prayer, and so Christians made pilgrimages to their tombs to pray, and seek spiritual strength. The early

Christians associated two realities with the shrines and tombs of the saints and martyrs—presence and power. As mentioned above, the saint or martyr is present not only at the site, but also in the worshipping community who gathers for prayer at the site. This is the reason why it is important to actually visit the sacred spot. It is this presence of the saints and martyr which draws people to shrines, tombs, and Churches that contain the relics or remains of them.

Besides presence, the power of the martyr or saint is what draws Christian pilgrims. The spiritual power to strengthen, heal, and edify the pilgrim is why they journey to Rome. These martyrs had given their lives for Christ; they had been imitators of him, to the point of shedding their blood for him. Certainly these "friends of Christ" are powerful intercessors for those who are still on earth. The martyrs and saints entered the transcendent realm of God. The prayers of the liturgies which are celebrated at the shrines or churches built over the tombs of the saints and martyrs are clear in expressing faith in this spiritual presence and intercession. Pilgrims come seeking spiritual help, and various types of healings: physical, spiritual, emotional, and psychological.

The main sites of Roman pilgrimage are the four major basilicas, which are the mandatory sites for a true Roman pilgrimage. The four are: St. Peter's, St. Paul's, St. John Lateran, and St. Mary Major. Every Christian pilgrim who journeys to Rome must visit at least these four churches.

Major Basilicas of the Jubilee Pilgrimage

When Pope Boniface VIII proclaimed the first Holy Year in 1300, he designated only two basilicas for the Jubilee pilgrimage. The basilicas of St. Peter and St. Paul were to be visited by pilgrims in the process of obtaining the Jubilee indulgence. In this way, Pope Boniface was promoting devotion to the two founders of the Church of Rome and institutionalizing the traditional pilgrimage *ad limina apostolorum.* The "trophies" of the Apostles were the sacred sites where the Jubilee graces were to be experienced most profoundly. The presence of the tombs of the Apostles gave the Church of Rome the *apostolicae plenitudo potestatis,* the "fullness of apostolic powers," according to Pope Boniface.

During the next Holy Year, in 1350 A.D., Pope Clement VI extended the Roman pilgrimage to the basilica of St. John Lateran. This basilica is actually the cathedral of Rome, and the Pope's church as the Bishop of Rome. Pope Clement recounted the Christian tradition that Pope Sylvester had baptized the Emperor Constantine in the Lateran basilica in the 4th century. And to add to the devotional aspect of the pilgrimage, the image of Savior, a precious icon of the face of Christ, was kept at the Lateran. This sacred image was kept in the Sancta Sanctorum chapel of the Popes at the Lateran and was believed to be a heavenly creation, "not made by human hands." Pilgrims during the Holy Year were to visit, then, three basilicas in their fulfillment of the Jubilee pilgrimage.

The next evolution in the Jubilee pilgrimage tradition was the inclusion of yet another basilica. For the Holy Year of 1390, Pope Gregory XI added the basilica of St. Mary Major. This basilica was built in honor of the Virgin Mary after the Council of Ephesus in 431 A.D., which proclaimed her the "Mother of God."

Pilgrim's Map from *Seven Churches of Christian Rome*,
by Antonio Lafrery, 1575 A.D.
Courtesy of Centro di Studi sulla cultura e l'immagine di Roma, Rome, Italy

Pope Gregory wanted to emphasize Mary's role in the plan of salvation. He also promoted the visit to St. Mary Major for the devotional reason of honoring the number of miracles that had taken place there as a result of her intercession.

This four-basilica pilgrimage has remained the standard route for pilgrims up until the present day. The path begins *ad limina apostolorum,* the basilicas of St. Peter and St. Paul, then on to the *Lateranensis ecclesia,* the basilica of St. John Lateran, and finally to the ancient Marian sanctuary of St. Mary Major. Since the Jubilee celebration of Pope Alexander VI in 1500 A.D., the inauguration of the Holy Year has been marked by the simultaneous opening of Holy Doors in all four of these basilicas with a solemn liturgical ceremony. Pilgrims during the Jubilee years enter the basilicas through these Holy Doors to symbolize the passage from sin into grace, forgiveness, and reconciliation.

The Artistic and Liturgical Heritage of Peter and Paul

In the ancient Christian imagination, the Apostles Peter and Paul, as founders and guardians of the Church at Rome, became the new "Castor and Pollux," the heavenly twin protectors of Rome according to Roman mythology. Later, they were also perceived as the new "Romulus and Remus," twin founders of the city of Rome, according to Roman legend. The joint martyrdoms of St. Peter and St. Paul became the new foundation upon which was built the spiritual reality of the new eternal "city set on a hill." The spiritual heritage of these Apostles became the principle of unity for the whole Church. Their mystical presence and power in Rome are the source of the pastoral responsibility and spiritual authority of the Church of Rome.

The parallelism of the two Apostles is demonstrated even in the monuments and art works of Rome itself. In St. Peter's Square, in front of the basilica, two enormous statues of St. Peter and St. Paul greet pilgrims on their way into the church. The two central medieval doors leading into St. Peter's basilica depict the martyrdoms of the Apostles in bronze relief. Inside the basilica of St. Paul, two statues of the Apostles are at the entrance to the sanctuary. And during the Renaissance, two statues of the Apostles were erected in the city. St. Paul's statue was placed on top of the ancient Column of the Roman Emperor Trajan, and St. Peter's statue was placed on top of the ancient Column of Emperor Marcus Aurelius.

Even earlier, in the apses of 4th-century basilicas in Rome, mosaics depicting St. Peter and St. Paul flanking Christ were common. In this ancient motif, Christ is enthroned in the New Jerusalem with St. Paul at his right hand and St. Peter at his left. This motif is often repeated in sculpture on early Christian tombs or *sarcophagi*. The two Apostles are depicted as flanking Christ, usually as representatives of the whole apostolic college of the Twelve. And quite often the martyrdoms of the two Apostles are depicted on these sarcophagi. The frescoes of the catacombs also give witness to the triad motif of Christ, St. Peter, and St. Paul.

The mystical presence and power of St. Peter and St. Paul in the Church of Rome is expressed not only in formal doctrine and in art, but also in liturgy. The belief and doctrine that St. Peter and St. Paul are the founders of the Church at Rome is celebrated liturgically. There are four celebrations in the Church's liturgical calendar which are connected to St. Peter and St. Paul.

The first is on January 25, the feast of the "Conversion of Paul." This feast day commemorates the conversion of Saul to St. Paul on the road to Damascus in Acts of the Apostles 9. It celebrates the privileged position of the apostle Paul in the life of the Church as one of the princes of the Apostles. The readings that day are from Acts of the Apostles and St. Paul's own writings. The Opening Prayer for that feast states, in part:

> *God our Father, you taught the gospel to all the world through the preaching of Paul your apostle. May we who celebrate his conversion to the faith follow him in bearing witness to your truth.*

The next celebration is on February 22, the feast of the "Chair of Peter." The image of the chair, or cathedra, is a symbol of teaching authority. This feast commemorates the role and authority of St. Peter as the supreme teacher of the Church. The Opening Prayer for the Mass of this feast states, in part:

> *All-powerful Father, you have built your Church on the rock of St. Peter's confession of faith. May nothing divide or weaken our unity in faith and love.*

170

On June 29, there is the solemnity of "Peter and Paul" which is a joint feast commemorating the witness of their martyr-doms. This feast is even a civic holiday in Rome, since it is the city of St. Peter and St. Paul. There are great festivities, parties, parades, and processions in Rome on this day. This is the most ancient and greatest feast day out of the four dedicated to St. Peter and St. Paul. The Preface for the Eucharistic Prayer for this Solemnity states, in part:

> *Father, all-powerful and ever-living God, we do well always and everywhere to give you thanks. You fill our hearts with joy as we honor your great apostles: Peter, our leader in the faith, and Paul, its fearless preacher. Peter raised up the Church from the faithful flock of Israel. Paul brought your call to the nations, and became the teacher of the world. Each in his chosen way gathered into unity the one family of Christ. Both shared a martyr's death and are praised throughout the world.*

This feast seems to have been connected with one of the Catacombs in Rome on the Appian Way, the Catacomb of St. Sebastian. There is a long tradition of venerating the two Apostles in the Catacombs at St. Sebastian. In fact, in ancient times, St. Sebastian was called the "Memorial of the Apostles." But if St. Peter and St. Paul's relics were in the graves inside the city, on the Vatican Hill and on the Ostian Way, then why did Christians go outside the city to these catacombs to show respect to their memory?

One theory states that during the persecutions of Emperor Valerian in the year 258 A.D., for fear that the apostles' tombs would be desecrated, the Christians secretly removed the bones of the apostles and placed them outside the city in the Catacombs of St. Sebastian. And then, when it was safe to move them back, they were transferred back to the Vatican Hill and the Ostian Way. This is known as the "translation theory." Tradition says that the bones were moved outside the city to these catacombs on June 29.

Finally, the fourth liturgical feast day on the Church's calendar is November 18, which is the feast of the "Dedication of the Churches of Peter and Paul." This feast commemorates the completion of Constantine's building project. When a church building is completed, it cannot immediately be used to celebrate the Eucharist. It must first be blessed and dedicated. This feast of November 18 celebrates the dedication of Constantine's two basilicas over the gravesites of the Apostles. The Opening Prayer for this feast states, in part:

> *Lord, give your Church the protection of the apostles. From them it first received the faith of Christ. May they help your Church to grow in your grace until the end of time.*

Not only are beliefs about St. Peter and St. Paul professed in doctrines and formal teachings, but also in art and in liturgies, the worship life of the Church. These four days on the Church's calendar are reminders of the importance and spiritual significance of the two Apostles even today as they continue to intercede and pray for the Church. These feast days are not just "history lessons," reminders of what these two did in the past, but they are opportunities for believers of today to ask St. Peter and St. Paul to intercede for, protect, and guide Christians in the present. They are even now praying for the Church, that it will be faithful to the teachings of Jesus and be his witness of truth, love and life in the world.

 ## Conclusion

Rome is the eternal city, the New Jerusalem, the city of St. Peter and St. Paul. Since the martyrdoms of the two apostolic founders, Rome has had a theological primacy among the various Sees of the Church, such as Antioch, Alexandria, Constantinople, or Jerusalem. This spiritual foundation of the Church of Rome, formed by the apostolic deposit of teaching and witness, has drawn Christian pilgrims to this city since the earliest days of the Church.

The "crossing of the threshold" into the third millennium is yet another opportunity to plummet the depths of the mystery of redemption. The power of this redemption is witnessed to by the faith, holiness, and heroic testimony of the Apostles, Martyrs, and Saints associated with the city of Rome. The wealth of this deposit of faith is made present and available to the pilgrim who journeys through the streets, squares, churches, and catacombs of Rome in search of deeper faith, hope, charity, and conversion of life.

Rejoice, O Rome, this day; thy walls they once did sign with princely blood, who now their glory share with thee. What city's vesture glows with crimson deep as thine? What beauty else has earth that may compare with thee? To God the three in One eternal homage be, all honour, all renown, all songs victorious, who rules both heaven and earth by one divine decree, to everlasting years in empire glorious" (Hymn for the Solemnity of Peter and Paul).

O noble Rome, ruler of the world, city without a peer, reddened with the crimson blood of martyrs, resplendent with the spotless purity of virgins. Till time is no more never shall we cease to greet and bless thee. Hail forever.

Peter, mighty holder of the heavenly keys, hear and grant the prayers of thy supplicants. And when you sit to judge the twelve tribes, be appeased and acquit us leniently. Have pity and help those who here below call upon thee thrice.

Paul, tireless vanquisher of worldly philosophies, give ear to our petitions. Now steward of the Divine munificence in the royal abode, sustain us so that through thy teaching the true wisdom which abounded in thee may overflow within us too" ("O Roma Nobilis," medieval pilgrims' hymn, XI–XII century).

FIVE

TRADITIONS AND CEREMONIES OF THE HOLY YEAR

Pilgrimage of Sign and Symbol

The history of the Holy Years bears witness to the fact that the pilgrimage to Rome became the foundation upon which all other Jubilee traditions and ceremonies were based. According to Pope Boniface VIII, the Jubilee indulgence could only be obtained by journeying to the threshold of the Apostles, *ad limina apostolorum,* the tombs of St. Peter and St. Paul. As the spirituality of the Jubilee pilgrimage developed, various devotional and penitential practices became associated with the sojourn to the eternal city.

The holy year pilgrim to Rome encounters the workings of God's grace through signs and symbols, liturgies and processions. The pilgrim experiences Jesus, the Word-made-flesh, through the tangible sights and sounds of the Jubilee traditions and ceremonies.

The phenomenon of pilgrimage is a type of incarnational spirituality in which the grace of God is encountered, as all five of the human senses are filled with impressions and experiences. The mystical dimension of these encounters is highlighted by the fact that the pilgrim is "surrounded by the great cloud of witnesses" (Hebrews 12:1) of the apostles, martyrs, and saints of Rome.

Some of the most important ceremonies and traditions which have evolved during the holy years would include the veneration of certain relics and devotional images, practices of hospitality for pilgrims, the Holy Door rituals, and processional visits to the major basilicas. These activities would complement the reception of the Jubilee indulgence.

Tradition of the Jubilee Indulgence

The theme of the Jubilee indulgence and its theology has been discussed above in Chapter One. This tradition changed the experience of the ancient pilgrimage to Rome, which had honored St. Peter and St. Paul, to a more penitential practice during the holy years with the purpose of obtaining the plenary indulgence.

The Jubilee 2000 spirituality of the indulgence is decidedly more biblical and grounded in the theology of redemption. The contemporary pilgrim is urged to live the Jubilee fully, that is, to open oneself to the dynamic of conversion and remove any spiritual obstacles which might hinder an intimate relationship with God. Repentance from sin and reconciliation with God and others form the basis of the modern notion of the Jubilee indulgence.

The proclamation of release and forgiveness in the tradition of the Jubilee indulgence is to be understood on both a spiritual and an ethical level. Forgiveness and remission of sins is to be accompanied by an awareness of the practical, moral implications of the grace of God in daily life. That is, the personal interior conversion of the believer must be manifested in outward attitudes and actions of social justice, as contained in the Old Testament theology of the Jubilee.

"The jubilee year was meant to restore social justice. The social doctrine of the Church, which has always been a part of Church teaching . . . is rooted in the tradition of the jubilee year" (TMA 13).

The spirituality of the Jubilee indulgence is to inform and determine the social, political, and economic dimensions of the Christian life. The advent of God's reign in the heart of the pilgrim through the gaining of the Jubilee indulgence is to be enfleshed in the midst of ordinary, temporal affairs of the world.

 ## Veneration of Relics and Devotional Images

From the very beginnings of the Jubilee pilgrimage to Rome, the veneration of relics and holy images has been part of the pilgrim experience. As mentioned above in Chapter One, the medieval tradition of the procession with Veronica's Veil through the streets of Rome during the Christmas season was one of the foundational elements of the very first Jubilee year in 1300 A.D. It was the great influx of pilgrims into

Rome for the procession with Veronica's Veil, and their desire for a plenary indulgence, which prompted Pope Boniface VIII to eventually declare a holy year.

The Veil of Veronica was displayed on Sundays at St. Peter's basilica during the medieval jubilee years. The spirituality and piety of the day emphasized the humanity of Jesus. As mentioned in Chapter Four above, another sacred image that was kept in Rome and on public display for pilgrims, was the image "not made by human hands" *Acheropita*. This was an ancient icon of the Savior, which was kept in the private Papal chapel at the Lateran palaces. It was considered to be a miraculous image imprinted by the Lord himself. By seeing the face of Jesus, icon of the Father, on the Veil of Veronica and the image "not made by human hands," the pilgrims entered into the mystery of the Incarnation in a profound way. Veneration of these important relics was part of a type of "theology of the face of God" which has its roots in the Old Testament.

The face of God in the Hebrew Scriptures was a metaphor of his presence among his people. Intimacy with God was characterized by seeing him "face to face." Beseeching God to show his face, particularly in the prayers of the Psalmist, expressed a desire for God to act within human history. "Rouse your power and come to save us. O Lord of hosts, restore us; if your face shine upon us, then we shall be safe" (Psalm 80:3–4).

Besides the community of Israel seeking God's presence in the events of history, the individual Jew also desired to experience

God's saving power in daily life. "Hear O Lord, the sound of my call; have pity on me and answer me. Of you my heart speaks; you my glance seeks; your presence, O Lord, I seek. Hide not your face from me" (Psalm 27:7–9).

The Jewish pilgrims in ancient Israel who journeyed to Jerusalem were seeking the face of God at Mount Zion.

Incision of St. Peter and St. Paul displaying the Veronica image, by S. Torello from the book Libro di Buona Compagnia, 1577 A.D.

Courtesy of Centro di Studi sulla cultura e l'immagine di Roma, Rome, Italy

Who can ascend the mountain of the Lord? Or who may stand in his holy place? He whose hands are sinless, whose heart is clean, who desires not what is vain . . . He shall receive a blessing from the Lord, a reward from God his savior. Such is the race that seeks for him, that seeks the face of the God of Jacob" (Psalm 24:3–6).

This theology of the face, rooted in the Old Testament, is brought to its fruition in Jesus, the icon of God, and the face of the Father. Veronica's Veil and the "image not made by human hands" represented, to the medieval pilgrims, an opportunity to behold the face of Him whom they hoped to see one day in Heaven. " when it comes to light we shall be like him, for we shall see him as he is" (1 John 3:2). This emphasis on incarnational spirituality is also at the heart of the Jubilee 2000 celebration.

"Christianity has its starting point in the incarnation of the Word. Here it is not simply a case of man seeking God, but of God who comes in person to speak to man of himself and to show him the path by which he may be reached. This is what is proclaimed in the prologue of John's gospel: 'No one has ever seen God; the only Son, who is in the bosom of the Father, he has made him known'(1:18)" (TMA 6).

Tradition of Hospitality for Pilgrims

Another tradition that developed as the history of the holy years unfolded was the practice of hospitality for pilgrims to Rome. Since the Jubilees were fundamentally pilgrimage feasts for the whole Church, practices of hospitality became very important. Hospitality for pilgrims had both a practical and spiritual value. Practically speaking, meeting the concrete needs of pilgrims to Rome made the daily logistics of the Jubilee more organized. And from a spiritual point of view, tending to the needs of pilgrims is a long-standing Biblical virtue that goes back to Abraham himself.

As early as the Holy Year of 1550 A.D., institutions and religious communities were organized for the sole purpose of tending to the needs of unprotected and homeless pilgrims during the Jubilee. St. Philip Neri was the first person to found a community and a hostel for pilgrims of his day. He erected a Confraternity dedicated to the "Most Holy Trinity" to tend to the needs of pilgrims and convalescents. This organized assistance consisted in provision of beds, food, baths, and accompaniment to the four major basilicas.

Members of the Confraternity of the Most Holy Trinity met the pilgrims at the ancient Milvian Bridge leading into the city of Rome. They brought the travelers to the pilgrims' hospice, washed their feet, and fed them. The pilgrims were given a freshly made bed and on the next day were provided with a type of picnic lunch and guided to the four major basilicas. In the evenings, the Confraternity provided concerts and preaching in the Church of the Most Holy Trinity, also built by St. Philip Neri.

Soon popes and queens would follow St. Philip Neri's example and engage in practices of Roman charity on behalf of the pilgrims. Many prominent religious and royal visitors to Rome for the Jubilee years would join the efforts of the Confraternity of the Most Holy Trinity in caring for pilgrims as a practice of humility and charity. For example, Pope Clement VIII, during the Holy Year of 1600 A.D., often invited twelve poor pilgrims to eat at his table and he personally waited on them. He visited the hostel of the Most Holy Trinity where he gave monetary contributions to pilgrims and personally washed the feet of pilgrims.

These practices of Roman charity find their source in the works of mercy of the Christian community and in the Bible itself. The Biblical virtue of hospitality is first demonstrated by Abraham in Genesis 18:1–15. Three heavenly visitors unexpectedly come to Abraham's tent in order to announce the birth of Isaac, the son of the promise. Abraham invites them to stay with him for a rest and offers to bathe their feet. When the angelic visitors agree to stay, he asks for the help of his wife Sarah and his servants in preparations for a lavish feast. During the meal, the Lord speaks through the heavenly visitors and delivers the message that Sarah will bear a son the following year. This is a fulfillment of God's promise to Abraham that he would be the father of a great nation.

The Genesis scene of the hospitality of Abraham for the three heavenly visitors has been interpreted by Christian scholars as a theophany, a manifestation of the Trinity to Abraham. It is a reminder that God is often disguised as guest and his presence is hidden in those who are in need of practical care and attention. Abraham offers hospitality and provides a model of charity and practical assistance for pilgrims. The three honored guests are portrayed as travelers, pilgrims who simply happen to pass by the tent of Abraham. And yet they are treated as royal visitors by Abraham who follows the ancient Oriental code of behavior for nomadic peoples. Every occasion of hospitality was to be approached as the "entertainment of angels."

In the New Testament, Jesus himself is a pilgrim-guest in the home of Martha and Mary in Bethany (Luke 10:38–42; John 11:1–44; 12:1–8). Journeying to the pilgrimage feast of Passover in

Jerusalem, Jesus stayed with these two sisters and enjoyed their practical hospitality and care. The experiences of table fellowship and pilgrim hospitality are sacred for both Judaism and Christianity. Abraham, Martha, and Mary share table fellowship with God himself. And in so doing, they provide a symbol and invitation for the sacred duty of hospitality. More than just a pious practice, hospitality and self-sacrifice for pilgrims is a privileged way of encountering the God who disguises himself as guest in the most unexpected ways.

5th century A.D. mosaic of "Hospitality of Abraham" from interior of Basilica of St. Mary Major, Rome, Italy

Courtesy of Basilica di Santa Maria Maggiore, Rome, Italy

God also plays the role of host to pilgrims. The risen Lord meets the two disheartened disciples on the road to Emmaus (Luke 24:13–35). The two travelers do not recognize the Lord until they are at table and Jesus breaks bread with them. This moment of Eucharistic insight of the risen Lord's presence takes place during an experience of table fellowship. Jesus is the host, who through word and sacrament invites the two pilgrim-disciples to encounter him in a new way—as risen from the dead.

The Jubilee 2000 is another opportunity for practicing hospitality towards pilgrims. Both the hosts and the holy year pilgrims are challenged to meet the God of the journey. Those who act as hosts are invited to experience God's hidden presence in the "least of these" whom they serve. And those who are pilgrim guests are exhorted to respond to the invitation of the God who serves.

"Who, in fact, is the greater—he who reclines at table or he who serves the meal? Is it not the one who reclines at table? Yet I am in your midst as the one who serves you . . . in my kingdom you will eat and drink at my table" (Luke 22:27–30).

Tradition of the Holy Door

Pope John Paul II envisions the Jubilee 2000 as literally a "threshold experience" leading the Church into the new millenium. The opening of the doors of human hearts to Christ has been a resounding theme of his pontificate. His very first message to the Church after being elected pope in 1978 was the call to "open wide the doors to Christ." The image of an open door is an evocative spiritual symbol. An open door symbolizes welcome, invitation, hospitality, and spiritual fellowship. "Here I stand, knocking at the door. If anyone hears me calling and opens the door, I will enter his house and have supper with him and he with me" (Revelation 3:20).

The archetype of the door is found even in pagan myth and symbolism. Doorways are, generally speaking, a prime imaginative form in the human psyche, and a fundamental form in the language of art. Doors symbolize transition from one state of being to another. A doorway can also be a basic theological principle because it connects two worlds. The passage over the threshold is a type of transit into a new spiritual sphere, usually characterized by rebirth.

The false doors constructed into ancient Egyptian tombs were thought to be symbols of entrance into the afterlife. And the ancient Romans often sculpted doors on the front of their large sarcophagi or marble coffins. These were also to be interpreted as symbols of entrance into the land of the dead, the afterlife.

According to Roman mythology, the Roman god Janus opened the gates of heaven when he went about his affairs in the morning, and closed them when he returned at night. Janus became the god of comings and goings, of entrance and exits, of doors, and gates, and passages. And in the Roman Forum, the doors of the temple of the god Janus were left closed or opened depending on whether the Roman Empire was at war or at peace.

In the Hebrew Scriptures, the image of the door, or gate of salvation, is a symbol of God's presence, healing, forgiveness, and liberation. The gates of Jerusalem on Mt. Zion were considered by ancient Jewish pilgrims as a symbol of entry into God's presence. "I rejoiced because they said to me, 'We will go up to the house of the Lord.' And now we have set foot within your gates, O Jerusalem" (Psalm 122:1–2). Isaiah's prophecy of the peace of the Messiah's future kingdom is described as a time when God's gates "shall stand open constantly; day and night they shall not be closed" (Isaiah 60:11).

The gates of paradise were barred after Adam and Eve were expelled from the Garden of Eden through sin (Genesis 3:24). But these gates of salvation are reopened through the Death and Resurrection of Jesus who opens the way to the Father (John 14:6). All who seek God through Jesus will have the door of salvation opened to them (Luke 11:9–10).

For Christians, the metaphor of the door or gate can be identified with Jesus himself. "I am the gate. Whoever enters through me will be safe. He will go in and out and find pasture" (John 10:9). He is the narrow door that leads to life (Matthew 7:14). The holy door of the Jubilee 2000 signifies God's mercy, open wide to all who seek and ask for it with a sincere heart.

The holy door of the Jubilee of the Year 2000 should be symbolically wider than those of previous jubilees, because humanity, upon reaching this goal, will leave behind not just a century but a millennium (TMA 33).

The tradition of the formal ritual opening of the holy door by the Pope himself can be traced back to 1500 A.D. and the Jubilee year of Pope Alexander VI. Alexander VI introduced the innovation of the opening of holy doors in all four of the major basilicas of Rome on Christmas Eve. The papal ceremony that was initiated in 1500 A.D. included a procession to the holy door of St. Peter's with the papal retinue, the wielding of a hammer by the pope making three ritual strikes on the door, a brief prayer, the lighting of candles, the crossing of the threshold, the singing of the *Te Deum*, and finally praying vespers inside the basilica. Today a collection of commemorative papal hammers

186

and trowels for the holy door ceremonies can be found in the Vatican Museum.

This elaborate papal rite replaced an earlier, much simpler rite of the opening of a door in the basilica of St. John Lateran, which had been used before 1500 A.D. The original holy door, it seems, was a door in the Lateran basilica known from ancient times as the "golden door." It was believed through pious legend that the image of the face of the Savior passed through this door and imprinted itself on the apse of the basilica. Perhaps as early as the Jubilee of 1350 A.D., the opening of this "golden door" at the Lateran and the crossing of its threshold by pilgrims was a holy year symbol of the passage from sin to a state of grace.

The tradition of crossing the threshold of the golden door of the Lateran basilica probably has its origins in earlier liturgical practices which used church doors in their rituals. In the early centuries of the Church, doors played a special role in liturgies and the practice of penance. For example, when the Eucharist was celebrated by the early Christians, a deacon would proclaim, "the doors, the doors." This was the cue for the doors of the church to be shut during the Eucharistic rite. The mystery of the Eucharist was not to be revealed to anyone who was not baptized. Therefore, the uninitiated were to be kept out of the church until they were received into the faith at the Easter Vigil.

The door of the church was also part of the rituals of Ash Wednesday at the beginning of Lent. The public penitents would be put outside of the door of the church and not allowed back inside until Holy Thursday when they were restored to the communion of the faithful. This practice reflects the idea of penance as an exclusion from holy places or a shutting out from the sacred mysteries. As Adam and Eve were expelled from paradise on account of sin, so too, the penitents were expelled from the church by literally having the doors of the church shut in their face.

After a season of repentance and penance, the penitents were reconciled back into the community in a Holy Thursday ceremony. The bishop would personally lead them by the hand back into the church. It seems clear, then, how the threshold of the church doorway became a symbol of forgiveness, healing, and reconciliation. "Open to me the gates of justice; I will enter them and give thanks to the Lord. This gate is the Lord's; the just shall enter it" (Psalm 118:19–20).

The symbolism of the holy door captured the imaginations of the medieval pilgrims. As a result, various stories and pious legends arose concerning these doors in the four major Roman basilicas. For example, one legend concerning the holy door of St. Peter's stated that it had been brought from the Holy Land. Allegedly, it was this door that Jesus passed through while bearing his cross on the way to Golgotha outside the walls of Jerusalem.

This particular legend probably had its origin in the stories that early Christian pilgrims brought back from the Holy Land. As mentioned above in Chapter Three, there was a gate in the walls of ancient Jerusalem known as the "golden gate." It was believed by the ancient Christians of Jerusalem that Jesus passed through this particular gate during his Palm Sunday entrance into the city. In the Middle Ages, this Jerusalem gate was only opened on Palm Sunday and the feast of the Exaltation of the Cross.

Once opened, the discarded bricks, mortar, and materials of this gate were considered to be prized relics for the medieval pilgrims to bring back to Europe. This tradition of the Golden Gate of Jerusalem seems to provide a rich analogy for the holy door in St. Peter's basilica. In fact, even before Pope Alexander VI in 1500 A.D., holy year pilgrims had great veneration for the masonry wall around the holy door of the Lateran basilica. When it was knocked down and the door opened, pilgrims scrambled to get a pieces of the wall as prized relics to be brought home.

Yet another strand of "holy door piety" associated the papal opening of the holy door with the figure of Moses. The ritual striking of the door with the hammer became a symbol of Moses striking the rock in the desert in order for the miraculous spring of water to flow (Exodus 17:5–6). The miraculous waters from the rock were understood as the streams of grace and pardon which flowed from the holy year door. "With joy you will draw water at the fountain of salvation" (Isaiah 12:3). This allusion to the figure of Moses was a connection with the Hebrew Jubilee traditions of the Old Testament.

On Christmas Eve, December 24, 1999, Pope John Paul II will open the great holy year door at St. Peter's basilica. The door will remain open throughout the celebration of the Jubilee 2000. One innovation concerning the other holy doors is that for the first time they will not be opened simultaneously with the papal opening of St. Peter's holy door. The holy doors of the other three Roman basilicas will be opened at other times for special celebrations.

The Four Basilica Pilgrimage

As mentioned above in Chapter Four, the Jubilee pilgrimage to Rome first included visits only to two basilicas, St. Peter's and St. Paul's, at the time of Boniface VIII in 1300 A.D. The number was soon increased to four by the addition of St. John Lateran and St. Mary Major. In the years 1600 and 1700 A.D., when floods barred access, and in 1825 A.D., when it was in ruins after a terrible fire, St. Paul's basilica was substituted by St. Mary's in Trastevere.

The four major basilicas are considered to be the "quadrangle" of Christian Rome. Each basilica has its own unique symbolism, history, and spiritual heritage. And yet there are some basic common elements they share. Each have sacred tombs, tall obelisk roadmarkers, and large plazas to accommodate feast day crowds. St. Peter's basilica is the symbol of Catholic unity. St. Paul's basilica is the symbol of Christian expansion and ecumenical fellowship. The basilica of St. John Lateran symbolizes the pastoral charity of the Roman Church. And the basilica of St. Mary Major symbolizes the presence of Mary, archetype of the Church, and Mother of the Church.

These basilicas are historical sites, important to the Christian tradition. At the same time, they are rich in works of art, architectural details, and devotional objects that attract the pilgrim's attention. Therefore this guide seeks to provide a spiritual key and a concise historical introduction to the visit of each basilica. It also aims at directing the pilgrim through the complex architectural and artistic environment of each basilica while keeping in mind the need for reflection and prayer.

The Jubilee pilgrimage to the four major Roman basilicas is a practical way of making concrete the fundamental concepts of the Christian message: conversion, self-denial, a sense of fellowship with other pilgrims, detachment from earthly things or temporal concerns, and the sense of being "on the way," encountering the God of the journey. In gaining the jubilee year indulgence, the pilgrim who visits the four basilicas is strengthened in Gospel values, challenged to live the reality of the communion of the faithful, and invigorated with a deep sense of mission.

Basilica of St. Peter

Liturgical Feast Days Associated with the Basilica – Chair of St. Peter, February 22, St. Peter and St. Paul, June 29, Dedication of the Basilicas of St. Peter and St. Paul, November 18.

This basilica, built over the tomb of the apostle Peter, calls the pilgrim to consider the witness of martyrdom for the sake of the Gospel. As mentioned in Chapter Four above, the joint martyrdom of St. Peter and St. Paul was interpreted by Patristic writers as the foundation of the Church at Rome. Their apostolic witness of teaching and preaching, along with their shed blood, is the mystical foundation of the primacy of Rome. The Pope, the bishop of Rome, is the successor of St. Peter and St. Paul. And the role of the Church of Rome is to continue this apostolic tradition of preaching, teaching, and Gospel witness.

History

The Apostle Peter was martyred on Vatican hill about 64–67 A.D. According to *Liber Pontificalis,* Pope Anacletus (79–91 A.D.) built an oratory over the tomb of the Apostle, near the Circus of Nero, but scholars are inclined to believe that this oratory was erected almost one century later by Pope Anicetus (155–166 A.D.). This shrine was known as a *Tropaion*—trophy of St. Peter, mentioned by the cleric Gaius around 200 A.D. This Tropaion was discovered during excavations under the floor of the modern building of the

Interior of Basilica of St. Peter
Courtesy of author Dr. Irena Vaisvilaite

Basilica. Around 320 A.D. on the site of the Tropaion, the Emperor Constantine began the construction of a basilica which was consecrated by Pope Silvester on November 18, 326 A.D.

When building the basilica the Emperor Constantine had to level the slope of the hill and to violate the immunity of the graveyard. Constantine's basilica was 120 meters long and 65 meters wide, with an impressive courtyard. The place of St. Peter's tomb was marked by a large marble cube with a canopy above it, supported by twelve columns. Over the years the basilica became enriched by many monuments, tombstones, frescoes, mosaics and statues and changed its appearance. But the most important site of the building, the pontifical altar over the tomb of the Apostle, was always in the center of the sanctuary and was always marked by a canopy.

In the fifteenth century, the building threatened to collapse and Pope Nicholas V (1447–1455 A.D.) began its restoration. After his death, the work was interrupted. Pope Julius II (1503–1513 A.D.) decided to reconstruct the basilica completely and commissioned a new project with the architect Bramante. His zeal to dismantle the old building and the destruction of many valuable historical details in the process, merited him the nickname Bramante Ruinante. Bramante's seeming lack of care about old St. Peter's might be explained by his desire to build over the tomb of the Apostle a real Martyrium. A Martyrium is a church over a martyr's tomb according to the tradition of the Christian East, and therefore Bramante envisioned a building with a Greek Cross floor plan, surmounted by a gigantic central dome.

After Bramante's death, a few famous artists like Rafael, Baltasare, Peruzzi and Antonio da Sangallo worked on the project. Some of them considered combining a Latin cross building, similar to old St. Peter's basilica, with a dome over the Apostle's tomb. In 1546 A.D., Michelangelo was appointed as St. Peter's architect and returned to Bramante's original idea. He created a massive Greek cross nave and an impressive cupola that was only half-finished at the time of his death in 1564 A.D. The dome was completed by 1590 A.D. According to the will of Pope Paul V, the nave towards the old square of St. Peter's was extended, transforming the building into a Latin cross, three-naved basilica with a dome over the monumental transept. The new facade of the basilica was built by the architect Carlo Maderna. This new church was consecrated by Pope Urban VIII on November 18, 1626 A.D., exactly 1300 years after the first consecration of the basilica.

In 1629 A.D., the architect and sculptor Gian Lorenzo Bernini was appointed as the Pope's architect. He created a newer and much larger canopy of gilded bronze over the tomb of the Apostle and an immense reliquary for the Chair of Saint Peter. Also, the square of St. Peter's is the work of this great Baroque artist.

The excavations, conducted in the 1940s and 1950s, uncovered under the floor of the basilica an ancient Roman necropolis and a very simple, shallow grave, covered with ceramic slabs. Around this grave are a number of other graves that crowd in on it, which shows the importance of the person buried inside. Behind the grave are two walls with graffiti invoking the intercession of St. Peter. Bones of an older man, wrapped in a purple cloth were found behind the second wall and were declared by Pope Paul VI as those of St. Peter. This excavation site may be visited if a private tour is arranged with the Scavi Office of the basilica.

Approaching St. Peter's

 Until modern times, the only way for pilgrims to access St. Peter's from the city was by crossing the Bridge of the Holy Angels—Ponte Sant' Angelo. This bridge is of ancient Roman construction, built by Emperor Hadrian (117–138 A.D.) to approach his mausoleum (now Castel Sant Angelo). For centuries this bridge was the only one that led to the Vatican hill from the center of Rome. Because of the importance of this bridge for pilgrimage to the tomb and to basilica of St. Peter's, Pope Clement VII in 1464 A.D. commissioned the artist Paolo Taccone to sculpt statues of St. Peter and St. Paul that were set on the end of the bridge. Two hundred years later, this bridge was embellished by Gian Lorenzo Bernini, who, with his helpers from 1668 to 1679, created five pairs of angels. Each angel holds a different symbol of Christ's Passion. So, the pilgrim, while still some distance away from St. Peter's, is already introduced to a meditation on Christ's Passion and on the witness given to the risen Lord by St. Peter and St. Paul.

The modern pilgrim might reach St. Peter's basilica in quite a few different ways and therefore miss the bridge of the Holy Angels. But it is impossible to miss the other introduction to St. Peter's basilica, which is the monumental Square of St. Peter's. It was also created by Gian Lorenzo Bernini. This square, according to the artist's intention, is meant to represent the loving embrace of the Mother Church and the semicircular colonnades that frame the square are intended as an image of arms, open wide to greet the pilgrim.

In the center of St. Peter's square stands an obelisk. This obelisk, dating from 1935 B.C. was brought to Rome from Egypt by the Emperor Caligula and installed in the Circus where later St. Peter is believed to have been martyred. This Circus was just behind the left side of the actual facade of the basilica and Pope Sixtus V in 1568 A.D. ordered the obelisk to be moved to its present site. This obelisk, which probably witnessed the martyrdom of St. Peter, was intended to symbolize the victory of Christ. Therefore, a relic of the true cross, enclosed into a bronze Cross, is installed on the top of the obelisk and the inscription on the base of the obelisk proclaims the victory of the Cross over the "adverse powers."

Bridge of the Angels, Rome Italy
Courtesy of author Dr. Irena Vaisvilaite

Two abundant fountains, set by Bernini at the sides of the obelisk, do not simply embellish the square, but are also reminiscent of the old custom of having a fountain in the courtyard of the ancient Christian basilicas. Such fountains (one was located in the courtyard of the old St. Peter's basilica) provided water both to quench thirst and to wash the dust of travelling. These fountains were also symbols of the living waters of salvation, that spring from the Cross of Christ.

The beautiful colonnades surrounding the square, and the covered galleries that connect these colonnades with the portico of St. Peter's, are topped by ninety-six statues of Saints and Martyrs, envisioning the triumphant Church in heaven. On the facade of St. Peters, over the entrance to the basilica, stand gigantic statues of Christ

St. Peter's Square
Courtesy of New Diacolor, Rome

along with statues of St. John the Baptist and the eleven Apostles (the statue of the twelfth apostle, St. Peter, is inside). Below the statue of Christ is a window and a balcony called the *Loggia delle bendizioni*. From this balcony the newly elected Pope gives his first address to the world. The solemn pontifical benediction known as the Urbi et Orbi—to the City of Rome and to the World—is granted from this balcony on the occasions of Christmas, Easter and some other important celebrations.

Entering Basilica

The symbolism of "Church," already extensively present in the square of St. Peter's increases even more when entering the basilica itself. After climbing the stairs that lead to the entrance of the basilica, pilgrims step into the Portico, which is the monumental Porch with five doorways. The vault of the porch is decorated with scenes from the Acts of the Apostles in the medallions. A lunette over the central door has a relief of "Jesus Christ entrusting His flock to Peter." Statues of thirty-six martyr-popes, represented in nineteen lunettes, are meant to indicate that the successors of St. Peter were ready to imitate Jesus, and to follow St. Peter himself, in shedding their blood for the flock.

The central bronze doors are from the old basilica of St. Peter's. They were commissioned by Pope Eugenius IV to the Florentine artist Filarette in 1439 A.D. The doors are decorated by reliefs, representing, from the top down, Jesus and Mary, St. Peter and Pope Eugenius and the scenes of martyrdom of St. Peter and St. Paul.

On the extreme right from the central entrance is the Porta Santa—the Holy Door that is opened only during the years of Jubilee. This door was given as gift to Pope Pius XII by Swiss Catholics in 1949 and was created by the artist Ludovico Consorti. Used as the Holy door for the Jubilee of 1950 and for the later Holy years, it illustrates the themes of forgiveness, pardon, reconciliation, and redemption. The two panels on the top left of the door show Adam and Eve expelled from Paradise and the two panels on the top right represent the Annunciation. The two left panels of the second row show Jesus' baptism and the finding of the lost sheep and the two right panels depict the prodigal son and Christ who cures the paralytic. In the third row from left to right are images of Christ forgiving the sinner, St. Peter asking how many times forgiveness must be granted, Christ forgiving St. Peter after his denial and Christ forgiving the Good Thief. In the lowest row these images follow: Thomas' unbelief, the institution of the sacrament of Penance, the conversion of St. Paul and Pope Pius XII opening the Holy Door of the 1950 Jubilee.

Baldacchino of St. Peter's
Courtesy of author Dr. Irena Vaisvilaite

Above the Holy Door on the left side is a large plaque with the text of Pope Boniface VIII's promulgation of the Jubilee year of 1300 A.D. When crossing the threshold of the basilica, the pilgrim is in the central nave of the enormous building, which tends to hide its real size. This impression is due to the Baldacchino—the majestic bronze canopy over the tomb of St. Peter that can be seen at the end of the central nave. This canopy immediately directs the attention to the place of the Apostle's tomb. It also visually frames the *Cathedra Petri* (St. Peter's Chair) with luminous glory at the

199

extreme end of the apse. By height, the Baldacchino is as high as the obelisk in St. Peter's Square (85 ft) and connects the horizontal and vertical directions in the basilica. In this way it moderates the impression of the overwhelming size of Michelangelo's dome. The true immensity of the building is revealed only as the pilgrim walks closer to the tomb of the Apostle. In the floor of the basilica, there are indications of the lengths of the world's largest churches, which enables the pilgrim to realize how enormous St. Peter's basilica really is.

This immensity of St. Peter's interior was poetically expressed by the German poet Schiller, who had the personified basilica address a pilgrim with these words:

> *Willst thou seek the immeasurable here?*
> *Then thou has erred,*
> *My greatness is*
> *To make greater thyself.*

The inscriptions in Greek and Latin running above the pilasters of the central nave describe St. Peter's mission in the Church. On the left is a quotation from Luke 22:32: "I have prayed for you, that your faith may not fail. You, in turn, must strengthen your brothers." On the left wall: "Whatever you bind on earth shall be bound in heaven; whatever you loose on earth shall be loosed in heaven" from Matthew 16:19. On the pillars of the central nave are one hundred and eight medallions of Saints and Martyrs, designed by Gianbattista Bernini. Fifty-six of these images are of early Popes, venerated as Saints. They were followers of St. Peter and with their very lives gave witness to the faith of Apostles.

Next to the last pillar on the right is a bronze statue of St. Peter. He is represented in ancient Roman fashion as a teacher. But instead of holding a scroll, which was typical for images of pagan philosophers and teachers, St. Peter holds the keys, which symbolize his spiritual authority. There are disagreements among specialists about the age of this statue. Some are inclined to date it from the 5th century A.D. or even earlier. But some insist that this statue is the work of the artist Arnolfo di Cambio, who lived in the 13th century. This statue was an object of reverence and devotion for pilgrims already during the first Holy Year of 1300 A.D. Most of pilgrims touch or kiss St. Peter's foot and then proceed to the tomb of the Apostle.

St. Peter's Tomb— *Confessio.* This Latin term indicates the grave of a confessor or a martyr, who confessed his faith by death. The grave of a martyr or a confessor is the place where "heaven and earth meet" and where the pilgrim should also confess his or her faith. On the balustrade of the Confessio are eighty-nine burning oil lamps which are also symbols of the light of faith.

Statue of St. Peter,
Basilica of St. Peter
Courtesy of author Dr. Irena Vaisvilaite

When looking down into the Confessio, the pilgrim can see two flights of stairs leading to the niche with the golden 9th century mosaic of the Savior. This niche coincides with the dimensions of the first monument on the tomb of St. Peter, the so-called Tropaion mentioned above. Pilgrims often mistake the gilded silver box in the niche for the reliquary containing St. Peter's remains. But this is not the case. In this box, the palliums, the special woolen stoles worn by Metropolitan archbishops, are kept until the feast of St. Peter and St. Paul, when the Pope bestows them on the shoulders of the new archbishops and patriarchs.

St. Peter's bones are behind the niche, in the wall that predates the time of Emperor Constantine, who had the remains of the Apostle removed from the original humble grave and immured in a hollow space within this wall. During the excavations in the 1940s and 1950s, archeologists discovered on this wall many inscriptions, invoking the prayers of Jesus, Mary and St. Peter. These inscriptions were left by ancient Christian pilgrims of the early centuries. In 1968, after a scientific examination of the bones, Pope Paul VI ordered them to be reenshrined. The original place of rest of the martyred body of Saint Peter may be seen on a guided tour of the excavations of the ancient cemetery which lies underneath the basilica.

Right above the place of St. Peter's grave is the papal altar and over it is the Baldacchino of Bernini. The actual altar was built by the will of Pope Clement VIII and dates from 1594. Within this altar the earlier altars of St. Gregory the Great (590–604 A.D.) and Pope Calistus II (1119–1124 A.D.) are enclosed.

When creating the four mighty columns of his Baldacchino, Bernini was inspired by the ancient twelve columns placed over St. Peter's tomb by Constantine, which were believed to be from the Temple of Jerusalem. Eight of the twelve original Constantinian columns now decorate the four balconies in the monumental piers of the Dome. Behind the balconies in the piers are chapels which contain the most important relics of St. Peter's basilica. These relics are: a piece of the true Cross given to the basilica by Pope Urban VIII; the lance of the Roman soldier Longinus, used to pierce the side of Jesus on the cross and given to Innocent VIII by Sultan Bajazet in 1489 A.D.; the Veil of Veronica, known to be in Rome from the 10th century and in the basilica from the year 1000 A.D.; and the head of the Apostle Andrew, brother of St. Peter, brought to Venice by Thomas Paleologos and given to Pope Pius II in 1462 A.D.

Pallium Niche
Courtesy of Reverenda Fabbrica di S. Pietro, Vatican City

The relics are indicated by the colossal statues below the chapels that contain them. St. Helena, the mother of Constantine traveled to the Holy Land in search of relics of the Passion of Christ and discovered the true Cross. The artist Andrea Bolghi depicts her holding the cross aloft.

St. Veronica was believed by popular piety of the Medieval age to be one of the weeping women met by Christ on his way to Golgotha. According to the pious legend, Veronica gave Jesus her veil to wipe his injured and bleeding face and this face became imprinted on the veil. The name "Veronica" probably comes from a compounding of the Latin attribute *vera* with the Greek word *ikon* which means a true icon, a true image of the Lord. According to the Medieval legend Veronica brought the veil to Rome and cured the emperor Tiberius from leprosy with it. Some scholars are inclined to relate Veronica with the Mandillion which was believed to be a relic of the true image of Jesus. According to the legend, this relic was given by Jesus himself to King Abgar of Edessa. This relic was known to be in Constantinople already in the 7th century. Soon after some true images of the Lord, "not made by human hands" appeared in Rome, in the Papal chapel in the Lateran. During the first holy year this relic was shown to the pilgrims in St. Peter's and became a symbol of Roman pilgrimages. The sculptor Francesco Mocchi represents St. Veronica holding the veil with the image of the Savior and hastening to tell others about it.

The Roman soldier Longinus, who, after witnessing the execution of Jesus became his follower, is imagined by Gianlorenzo Bernini as gazing upwards, toward the cross that crowns the Baldacchino. St. Andrew, sculpted by Francois Duquesnoi, embraces the cross of his martyrdom with visible enthusiasm. In such a way the tomb of St. Peter is surrounded by memories and symbols of the Lord's Passion to which St. Peter, as well as the other Apostles and Martyrs, gave witness.

Above the piers runs an inscription indicating St. Peter as the source of unity in the Church: "Thus, one faith shines in the world, thus, one priesthood arises." Medallions with mosaic images of the four evangelists, Matthew, Mark, Luke and John, symbolizing the Gospel tradition, are in the pendantives above the piers that sustain the Dome, resplendent in gold mosaics.

Statue of St. Veronica
Basilica of St. Peter.
Courtesy of author Dr. Irena Vaisvilaite

The Dome soars directly above the Tomb of St. Peter. Decoration of the dome is made in such way that St. Peter and his ministry and, through it, the history of all the Church is represented as part of the history of salvation. The vertical lines of the double pilasters in the drum of the Dome drive up until they converge at the lantern. God the Father with his arms outstretched in blessing and benediction is here represented. The sixteen compartments of the Dome are decorated with figures of the angelic orders. Above the windows are figures of Jesus, Mary, St. John the Baptist, the twelve Apostles and St. Paul. Below, on the base of the drum of the Dome runs the inscription—"You are Peter, and upon this rock I will build my church. I will give you the keys to the kingdom of heaven" from Matthew 16:18.

The Dome, which is a beautiful symbol of God's mercy, was designed by the elderly Michelangelo, who refused payment for this work, because, in his words, this was a contribution "to God's Glory." The creator of the Dome's decoration was the 16th century artist, Cavalier d'Arpino.

God the Father, portrayed in the lantern of the dome, is the origin of salvation history, which unfolds in the life, Death, and Resurrection of the Son. This mystery is expressed in the Gospel apostolic tradition and given witness in the martyrdom and the ongoing Petrine ministry in the Church. The dome, baldacchino, confessio, and tomb of St. Peter are, all together, an organic artistic and symbolic catechesis of God's plan of redemption.

In the apse of the basilica, the pilgrim can see the *Cathedra Petri,* the Chair of Peter, which symbolizes the Pope's teaching office. This Cathedra was created by Bernini as a giant reliquary which contains an old wooden throne with ivory inlays, believed to be the chair used by St. Peter himself as bishop of Rome. Scientific examination ordered by Pope Paul VI revealed, however, that this throne is actually from the ninth century and was used in 875 A.D. for the coronation of the Frankish emperor Charles the Bald, who gave it to the Pope John VIII. This precious throne was used by Popes for solemn events and became, in popular imagination, the throne of St. Peter himself.

Pope Alexander VII commissioned Bernini to make a fitting container for this relic. Bernini's work was unveiled on

January 17, 1666. The composition, in which the artist freely used various materials, is one of the most outstanding works of the Baroque style. The gilded bronze chair seems to be floating in the air. The scene of Jesus entrusting St. Peter with his flock ("Feed my lambs") is carved on the back of the chair. Four Doctors of the Church, two from the East (Athanasius and John Chrysostom) and two from the West (Augustine and Ambrose) are graciously touching the legs of the throne. Above is a stained glass window with the image of a Dove. This symbol of the Holy Spirit, surrounded by clouds and angels, makes visible the idea of the presence of the Spirit in the Church. This throne is symbol of the office of St. Peter, and it interesting that there is no permanent bishop's chair or cathedra in this basilica. One is temporarily placed next to the papal altar only when the Bishop of Rome celebrates Eucharist here. On February 22, when the western Church commemorates the feast of the Chair of St. Peter, seventy two burning candles are placed on the *Cathedra Petri,* symbolizing the seventy two disciples of Christ, sent by him on mission into the world in Luke 10:1.

Chair of Peter, Cathedra Petri, by Bernini, Basilica of St. Peter

Courtesy of Dr. Irena Vaisvilaite

In the naves of the basilica, numerous tombstones of Popes of different times are found. Additional papal tombs, as well as remnants of the old Constantinian basilica and various chapels, can be seen by the pilgrim when descending to the Grotte Vaticane, the Vatican Grottos. The entrance to this lower level of St. Peter's is behind the statues in the piers of the dome. This is one of the possible ways to exit the basilica. But before exiting, the pilgrim might return to the entrance where to the leftside of the Holy Year door is a chapel with Michelangelo's Pieta, which is the world famous work of the young sculptor who created a beautiful meditation on hope when all hopes are gone. The Mother holds on her lap the body of her dead son and still, in the midst of terrible suffering, accepts God's will. Before reaching this chapel the pilgrim might like to stop in the Chapel of the Blessed Sacrament, reserved for prayer and silence.

Reflection

The tomb of St. Peter, under the main altar of the basilica, reminds the pilgrim of the words of Jesus in Matthew 16, "Peter, . . . You are rock, and upon this rock I will build my Church . . ." and in John 21, "Feed my sheep . . . when you are older you will stretch out your hands and be led to where you do not want to go . . . ." These words of commissioning find their fulfillment and fruition in the supreme act of St. Peter laying down his life for the sake of the sheep, the Church. In carrying out the papal ministry, the bishop of Rome is to be the chief shepherd of the flock of God. This shepherd is to nourish, care for, defend, guide, and if need be, lay down his life for the sake of the sheep. As 1 Peter states, the shepherd is also to be the guardian against distortions of the Gospel. And in a preeminent way, the Pope is to follow the example of St. Peter as a harmonizer of various trends, dimensions, and interpretations of the Christian tradition. The book of the Acts of the Apostles portrays St. Peter as a source of reconciliation, a point of reference, and a figure committed to unity in the early Christian community. This witness of St. Peter is actualized in the Church of Rome through the ongoing power and presence of the Holy Spirit in the midst of the Christian community.

The humble tomb of the Fisherman from Galilee, called to proclaim the Good News, is in the center of the enormous space of St. Peter's basilica, which serves also as a necropolis of many bishops of Rome. Meant as a monument to the power of Popes over the nations, this basilica, filled with people of all languages and races, now exalts the mission of evangelization and of charity. This mission of service of the Church is indicated also by the statues of founders and foundresses of religious orders and important spiritual movements, which are placed in the niches of the piers of central nave. It is worth remembering that the Second Vatican Council, which called for renewing the pastoral work and mission of the Church, was held in this nave.

The pilgrims who visit this basilica are challenged to consider the faith of St. Peter as a model for their own Christian journey. St. Peter is presented in the Gospels as an impetuous, sometimes bumbling, follower of Jesus. But what is strikingly disarming about St. Peter is his big-heartedness and his deep love for his Lord. Despite his foibles and mistakes, what shines forth from his rough and ready fisherman character is a genuine affection for Jesus, and a commitment to the kingdom of God. St. Peter's intimacy with Jesus, even after the Passion story when he denied knowing Jesus three times, is a challenge for ongoing conversion for every Christian. His reconciliation with Jesus after the Resurrection is a model for the believer who seeks reconciliation and renewal by making a pilgrimage and encountering the God of the journey. Not only is the Church of Rome and the Pope to continue St. Peter's agency of reconciliation, but also the pilgrim who prays at the threshold of the tomb of the apostle in this magnificent basilica. Edified through the witness of St. Peter, the pilgrim is enabled to grow into an agent of reconciliation in the family, community, workplace, and world.

 ## Basilica of St. Paul's Outside the Walls

Liturgical Feast Days Associated with the Basilica—the Conversion of St. Paul, January 25, St. Peter and St. Paul, June 29, Dedication of the Basilicas of St. Peter and St. Paul, November 18.

This basilica, built over the tomb of the apostle Paul, also calls the pilgrim to consider the witness of martyrdom for the sake of the Gospel. As the patristic writer Tertullian stated, "...the apostles poured forth their whole teaching, along with their blood into the Church of Rome . . ." Like St. Peter, the apostle Paul culminates his ministry of the Word with the spiritual victory of winning the crown of martyrdom. As he states in 2 Timothy, ". . . the time for my departure is near, even now my life is being poured out as an offering. I have fought the good fight, I have finished the race, and now what awaits me is a crown of glory that will never fade, life on high in Christ Jesus . . ." (4:6–8).

According to Acts of the Apostles 23:11, while St. Paul was sitting in a prison cell in Jerusalem, the risen Lord appeared to him and said that he must give testimony to him in Rome. And by the end of the book, in Acts 28:30–31, St. Paul is in the city of Rome under house arrest, able to receive guests and stay in communication with the communities he had founded, bearing witness to the Gospel. Although St. Paul's martyrdom, like St. Peter's, is not mentioned in the New Testament, the evidence of Patristic writers testifies to his execution outside of the walls of Rome on the road leading to the port city of Ostia. St. Paul was beheaded on the Ostian Way in the place "by aquae Salviae" and his body was buried, according to tradition, by a pious Roman matron named Lucina, in a nearby pagan cemetery. Today the magnificent basilica of St. Paul's Outside the Walls stands over the site of his grave.

Approaching the Basilica of St. Paul's Outside the Walls

When traveling to St. Paul's Outside the Walls, the pilgrim must leave the territory of the ancient city of Rome. The old Ostian road, which once ran in the middle of fields, now goes through a busy modern neighborhood. St. Paul's basilica appears in the middle of the busy and congested surroundings, separated from the outside world by the monumental

Quadriportico or courtyard, formed by four colonnades. When approaching the basilica from the city, it is possible to see, on the left side of the road, not far from the bell tower of the basilica, the covered excavations of the cemetery, called "in predio Lucinae" or "Sepolcreto Ostiense." This is a part of the cemetery in which St. Paul was buried. From the side of this excavation runs the road of the Seven Churches—*via delle Sette Chiese*. This was a pilgrim's way that connected the site of St. Paul's tomb to the catacombs and the Basilica of St. Sebastian.

History

Around 324 A.D., the Emperor Constantine replaced the small oratory of the 2nd century, known as the *caella memorie* of St. Paul on the Ostian way, with a basilica and placed the body of the Apostle in a bronze sarcophagus with a marble slab over it. In 384 A.D. enlargement of the basilica began and was completed under the emperor Theodosius (395–493 A.D.). The building was further embellished by Pope Leo III (795–816 A.D.) and became, together with St. Peters, one of the two largest churches in Rome. In 847 A.D. the basilica was pillaged by Saracens and then repaired by Pope John VIII. Restored a few more times, it survived until July of 1823 A.D. when was it was in great part destroyed by a fire. Reconstruction was a long process and was only partially concluded in 1854 A.D., when the new building was consecrated by Pope Pius IX, in the presence of one hundred and eighty seven bishops, who had gathered in Rome on the occasion of the solemn proclamation of the Dogma of the Immaculate Conception. The present basilica is the same in size and plan as the one that was destroyed.

This basilica has a special connection with England and with the ecumenical efforts of the Catholic Church. Before the Reformation, the King of England was ex-officio a canon of St. Paul's. In 1966, Pope Paul VI and the Archbishop Ramsey of Canterbury celebrated a service of prayer here and issued a joint declaration of amity. Since then the Closing of the Week of Prayer for Christian Unity is celebrated in St. Paul's Outside the Walls, perhaps symbolizing the ecumenical and all-inclusive nature of St. Paul's mission.

Quadriportico

Before the entrance of the original basilica there was a spacious atrium with a fountain in the center. The present Quadriportico dates from 1885–1929 A.D., and follows the form of an old fourcourt and is surrounded by a colonnade of one hundred and forty six granite columns. While closely imitating in size and shape the Quadriportico of the old Basilica, it lacks an important element, namely, a fountain for ablutions. The fountain for pilgrims is substituted by the statue of St. Paul. The inscription at the base of the statue reads: "To the preacher of the Truth, the teacher of the nations." St. Paul is represented as a traveler, with his head covered. He holds a sword which was the instrument of his martyrdom and a symbol of the word of God that he preached (Hebrews 4:12).

Façade

On the façade of the ancient basilica was a mosaic with solemn images of St. Peter and St. Paul. The modern façade mosaic (1854–1874 A.D.) by Filippo Agricola, follows early Christian examples and represents Christ, seated on a throne. Beneath this the Mystical Lamb stands on a mound, from which flow the four rivers of Paradise. Twelve sheep, symbolizing the Apostles and therefore the whole Church, approach him from the two cities— Jerusalem and Bethlehem, the sites of the Birth and Death of Jesus. Between the windows are the four major Old Testament prophets, Isaiah, Jeremiah, Ezekiel and Daniel. Under the portico, the wall niches have statues of St. Peter and St. Paul.

The central door was made in 1931 A.D. by the Florentine artist, Antonio Maraini. When the door is closed, the pilgrim might see the impressive feature of the Cross, highlighted in silver. The names of the four evangelists and images of the twelve apostles are represented on this cross. Panels on the left depict the scenes of the life of St. Peter and those on the right of St. Paul. A silver figure of Jesus indicates the scenes of the vocational calling of both apostles. In such a way, as in the decoration of St. Peter's basilica, the ministries and the martyrdoms of St. Paul and St. Peter are represented as basic to the identity of the Church of Rome.

Basilica of St. Paul, Rome
Courtesy of New Diacolor, Rome

On the right from the central door is the Holy Door. This bronze door was the main door of the old basilica and is the work of two artists, Theodoros and Staurachios, who made this door in Constantinople in the year 1070 A.D. for Hildebrant, the abbot of St. Paul's. The year 1054 A.D. is commonly accepted as the date of the Great Schism or split between the Western and Eastern Churches. The Schism was due to some liturgical and disciplinary disagreements that ended in the exchange of excommunications between the Papal legates and the Patriarch of Constantinople. This door of St. Paul's is one of many indications, that neither side considered the split serious a short time afterwards. The real division of Eastern and Western Christianity was determined by a slow cultural isolation and estrangement and the separated lives of the Churches through the centuries. The Holy Door of St. Paul's is therefore perceived in present times as a symbol of hope for the rapprochement of these two great Christian traditions and of all ecumenical movement. Unlike the Holy door of St. Peter's basilica, that will be opened on the Solemnity of Christmas of 1999, the Holy door of St. Paul's Outside the Walls will be solemnly opened on January 18, 2000, the beginning of the Week of Prayer for Christian unity.

Interior

The inner space of St. Paul's is an excellent example of an early Christian basilica. The forest of columns divide the church into five naves, the central one being higher than the side ones. This space gives a good indication about the size and appearance of early churches in Rome. The basilicas built by Constantine and later emperors were conceived for the gathering of the entire community for Eucharist. During the offertory, this community would move toward the altar, which demanded that the central nave be large and free from obstacles.

Above the columns of the naves run rows of Papal portraits. It is interesting that the chronology of the popes from St. Peter to the most recent Pontiff was and is here, which indicates again the Pauline dimension of the ministry of the bishop of Rome. As successor of St. Peter and St. Paul, the bishop of Rome is to continue the ministry of St. Paul in an ardent zeal for the promotion of the good news of Christ. As an aggressive missionary of the Gospel to all peoples, the Pope labors to free the message of Jesus from any cultural restraints or encumbrances, as St. Paul did. In this way, the embrace of the Christian message by everyone everywhere is a goal to be striven toward through the teaching and preaching of the Church of Rome. As St. Paul exhorts in his Letters, a pastor is also to encourage, test, and coordinate all the various charisms and ministries of the members of the Church. This role helps to ensure that the life of the Church, as manifested in a diversity of gifts and vocations, reflects the fullness of the Body of Christ in all its members.

In the old basilica, the pontifical portraits were painted, and the few that survived the flames of the nineteenth century fire are in the basilica's museum. The new portraits are made in mosaic. The windows of the naves are made from alabaster, which provides warm, golden light. The central nave is ended by the triumphal arch, which frames the altar area. The mosaic of this arch is from the 5th century and was commissioned, as the inscription at the bottom of it says, by Galla Placidia (386–450 A.D.), sister of Emperor Honorius. The triumphal arch exalts Christ—the greatest victor who through his Death and Resurrection conquered sin and Death. Christ is represented at the center of the mosaic within a circle, holding a shepherd's staff. His face is solemn and severe. The twenty-four elders, as described in the Book of Revelation (Revelation 4:10), hold their crowns in honor of Christ. The arch is an image of the ultimate victory of Christ, and of his Second Coming. St. Peter and St. Paul are below the elders and are giving their testimony to Christ's victory. Behind the arch is the tomb of the apostle Paul, who with his life and death testified to the risen Lord. So, the triumphal arch over the tomb of a martyr reminds the pilgrim that the tomb is a site of spiritual victory and, like Jacob's Ladder (Genesis 28:12, 17), it is a meeting place of heaven and earth. The tomb site itself, then, is an eschatological reality.

St. Paul's tomb is below the altar, behind a grill, where a small red light burns constantly. If peered at through the grill, it is possible to see the marble cover of the sarcophagus with the inscription: "To Paul, Apostle and Martyr." The cover has holes, made for direct contact with the inside of the tomb. Through these holes, in ancient times, pilgrims were able to lower down objects to touch the sarcophagus of the Apostle. And these pieces of cloth became prized relics for the ancient pilgrims.

Above the tomb rises the splendid canopy, the work of Arnolfo di Cambio, supported by four porphyry columns. At the four corners of the canopy are statues of St. Peter, St. Paul, Paul's disciple Timothy, and of the Benedictine abbot Bartholomew, who commissioned this work, that dates from 1285 A.D.

The apse of basilica is decorated with ancient marbles that survived the 19th century fire. The Apse mosaic dates from 1220 A.D. and is the work of Venetian artist Pietro Zani. After the fire, a serious restoration work was done on this mosaic that represents Christ on a cushioned throne, similar to those of Byzantine emperors. Like an Emperor, Christ is dressed in purple and gold. He holds a book with the words: "Come blessed of my Father and receive the kingdom prepared for you" (Matthew 25:34). This image, as the one on the triumphal arch, is eschatological, showing the coming of *kairos,* or God's time. It symbolizes the day when Christ will come to bring human history to a close and fully inaugurate his kingdom. At the right hand of Christ stand St. Paul and St. Luke, and at the left, St. Peter and St. Andrew. The palm trees symbolize the life in paradise. Below Christ's figure on the lower level is an image of a jeweled cross on a throne with the symbols of the Passion. This throne is flanked by the figures of angels and apostles.

At the right side from the canopy is the Easter candlestick *(candelabrum)* from 1170 A.D. This magnificent work of Roman marble was crafted by Nicola d'Angelo and Pietro Vassaleto. It is 18 feet high and gives a glimpse of the medieval Eastern liturgy. The trunk of candlestick is subdivided into six horizontal sections that contain scenes from the life of Christ being led to Caiaphas and Pilate, his derision, Crucifixion and Resurrection. The candelabrum was placed here after the fire, but its presence, as with all the decoration surrounding St. Paul's tomb, highlights his martyrdom as part of Christ's Easter victory and therefore of the new Creation (Isaiah 65:17–25).

Reflection

The pilgrims who visit this basilica are challenged to consider the witness of St. Paul as the great apostle to the Gentiles, a zealous missionary for Christ. St. Paul is celebrated as one of the great converts to Christianity. Trained as a Pharisee, and fiercely committed to the Jewish Law and way of life, Saul of Tarsus persecuted the infant Church. But as the book of Acts of the Apostles reports, he was stopped in his tracks on the road to Damascus by a vision of the risen Lord. This encounter with Jesus, who identified himself with the Church, " I am Jesus, whom you are persecuting . . ." (Acts of the Apostles 9: 4–5) proved to be the turning point in his life. With his conversion to Christianity, he brought his great love of the Scriptures and his keen mind to the task of preaching and teaching the message of Jesus.

St. Paul is presented by Acts of the Apostles and his own Letters as an evangelist who utilizes every opportunity in his life, including sufferings and disappointments, as an occasion to share the good news of Christ with others. This high-powered and well-respected Pharisee turned impoverished and humble Christian preacher, who fails at Athens and is arrested, beaten and imprisoned several times, learns through his sufferings that when he is weak, then he is strong (2 Corinthians 12:9–10). The power of the

Cross shines through St. Paul, it seems, when he is at the point of greatest vulnerability. The success of his ministry and the growth of the churches he has founded depend not on him but on the risen Lord who met him on the road to Damascus and

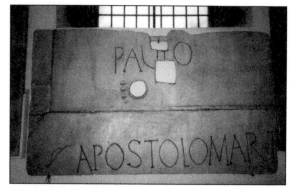

Copy of the marble slab cover over the tomb of St. Paul, Pinacoteca Museum, Basilica of St. Paul Outside the Walls

Courtesy of author Dr. Aurelie A. Hagstrom

continues to lead him on his missionary adventures. Ironically, the young Pharisaic intellectual who previously avoided any contact with non-Jews, so as not to risk ritual impurity, now finds himself called by God to be an apostle to the Gentiles and become a pilgrim for the sake of the Good news. His example inspires those who hear the call to conversion to begin their pilgrimage of faith.

The first chapel to the left of the apse is the Chapel of the Blessed Sacrament. This Chapel is related to the two great pilgrim-saints in Rome—Saint Brigid of Sweden, who came to Rome during the Jubilee of 1350 A.D. and Saint Ignatius Loyola, who was present in Rome when returning from his pilgrimage to Jerusalem. The crucifix over the altar is said to be the one that spoke to St. Brigid when she prayed in this basilica. The statue of the kneeling Brigid is by Stefano Maderno. In this chapel in 1541 A.D., St. Ignatius Loyola and his friends took their corporate oath formally establishing the Society of Jesus. In the niche on the right of the crucifix is the ancient statue of St. Paul, damaged by fire and by pilgrims, who used to take pieces of its wood as relics from this basilica.

At the far right end, when facing the apse, is the exit to the courtyard of the Benedictine monastery, which is adjacent to the basilica. It is also possible to visit the small museum, which holds remains from the old building and some valuable paintings. The courtyard was built by Pietro de Maria, and his father Pietro Vassalletto, who made the Easter candelabrum. The walls of the courtyard have fragments from the monuments and sarcophagi from the ancient necropolis under the basilica's floor. Some of the tombstones are pagan, while others bear signs of the Christian faith.

The monastic courtyard is meant to symbolize paradise. It has a cruciform walk to the center, where there is a fountain, reminding the pilgrim of the fountain of living water (John 7:37–39). The perimeter walkways are delimited by a podium with pairs of columns and other sustaining columns. The pediment on the top is decorated with mosaics, as well as columns of the northern side of the walkway. This richness of decoration enhances the symbolism of the courtyard.

On the left side of the Courtyard are two entrances leading to the Pinacoteca, or small museum of the basilica. Here on the wall is a copy of the marble cover of the Apostle Paul's tomb and four examples of papal portraits from the ancient basilica are exposed.

Reflection

The passion of St. Paul's preaching is matched by the skillfulness of his intellect in explaining the truths of the Christian faith to others. The pilgrim who prays at his tomb in this basilica is confronted with the same challenge of being committed to evangelization through word and deed to people of all cultures, races, and creeds. Through the meditation on Scripture that a pilgrimage affords, the believer is strengthened in the call to be a missionary in daily life. St. Paul's insight of the power and freedom that the grace of God brings to the life of the believer is an inspiration for all who seek to experience the dynamism of the Holy Spirit. Edified by this Spirit-filled herald of the Gospel, the pilgrim is enabled to grow as a courageous witness to the truths of the faith, which flow from the saving power of the dying and rising of Jesus.

 ## Basilica of St. John Lateran

Liturgical Feasts Days Associated with the Basilica—the Birth of St. John the Baptist, June 24, the Beheading of St. John the Baptist, August 29, The Dedication of St. John Lateran, November 9, St. John the Evangelist, December 27.

The Basilica of St. John Lateran calls the pilgrim to consider the witness of St. John the Baptist, herald of the coming of the Messiah. St. John was the voice crying out in the wilderness, a prophetic figure announcing the coming of the anointed one of God. He represents the end of one age and the beginning of another. In St. John's mission, the Old Testament period comes to a close, and the New Testament begins. He is a sort of clasp between the testaments, styled as an Old Testament prophet; he inaugurates the new age of God's unfolding plan of salvation (Mark 1). This basilica, although not built over the tomb of a martyr or saint, still preaches the Gospel message by reminding the pilgrim of the one who recognized Jesus as the Lamb of God who would take away the sins of the world (John 1:36). As St. John the Baptist proclaimed his awareness of Jesus, so too, the pilgrim is challenged to come to a deeper understanding of the identity of Jesus, who is the same yesterday, today, and forever.

Interestingly, this basilica, which is the cathedral for the diocese of Rome, was not originally dedicated to St. John the Baptist. The oldest title for this church is the basilica of the Holy Savior. The magnificent image of the Savior can be seen in the apse mosaic of the fourth century. It was perhaps one of the first public images of Jesus to be displayed, considering that it was one of the first basilicas built and adorned by the Emperor Constantine after his conversion to Christianity. This bearded Christ with dark, medium-length hair parted in the middle became a type of model for future artistic images of Christ. The early Christians in the Roman church were so impressed by this image, that a legend arose stating that the Lord himself imprinted this image on the apse of the basilica while the building was under construction.

History

The cathedral of Rome owes its origin to the gift of land and property on the outskirts of Rome, given by the emperor

Constantine to Pope Melchiades (311–314 A.D.). This territory in earlier times was the property of an influential Roman family, Laterani, who gave the name to the place. The basilica was consecrated in the year 342 A.D. and dedicated to the Holy Savior. At the same time the Baptistery was built and consecrated, and the palace of the Popes, called *Episcopium* and later *Patriarchium* was erected. Popes resided here until 1304 A.D., when they went to Avignon, and in 1377 A.D. the popes returned to the territory of the Vatican.

In the ninth century, Pope Sergius III dedicated the basilica also to St. John the Baptist and in the twelfth century Pope Lucius II added the name of St. John the Evangelist. The one chapel adjacent to the Baptistery received the same dedication. The Lateran Basilica, as the Popes cathedral, was of the highest rank in the city. Its importance was highlighted by the inscription on the facade, that stated that by the will of the Pope and of the Emperor this temple shall be considered the head and the mother of all churches. From 1123 to 1215 A.D. five ecumenical councils were held in the Lateran. One more council was held between 1512 A.D. and 1517 A.D.

The first Lateran basilica consisted of five naves, separated by rows of columns and decorated by marbles and mosaics. The building suffered much from invasions, fires, and earthquakes and very little of the original building has survived to present times. Since this basilica is not built over the tomb of a martyr or saint, in medieval times, the faithful came to believe that the heads of St. Peter and St. Paul were transferred here by Constantine. It was also believed that Helena, mother of Constantine, brought to the basilica from Jerusalem the table of the Last Supper. Due to this tradition, on Holy Thursday, the Mass of the Last Supper is celebrated in the Lateran basilica. The old Roman tradition also states that in the altar of the basilica is a relic of the table from the house of the Roman patrician Pudentius. St. Peter is supposed to have been a guest there and to have celebrated the Eucharist on this table.

In different times various additions and changes were made for embellishment or sometimes for repair of this ancient and very important building. A radical transformation was undertaken by the initiative of Pope Innocent X (1644–1655 A.D.) for the Jubilee of 1650 A.D. The Pope entrusted the famous artist and architect Francesco Borromini for the reconstruction of the basilica's interior. The exterior was modified by the architect Alessandro Galillei in 1735 A.D. The altar area was renovated by the will of Pope Leo XIII, in 1885 A.D.

Approaching St. John Lateran

The Lateran is no longer located on the outskirts of Rome as it was for centuries, when fields and some country houses surrounded the monumental complex. The basilica is now trapped in one of the busiest traffic routes of Rome.

Some of the imperial city walls have survived and, if the pilgrim is coming from the catacombs on the Appian Way, when crossing Porta San Giovanni (St. John's Gate) the basilica is seen in the solemn beauty of the principal facade. Also, those who approach the Cathedral of Rome from the side of the city are given a monumental view of the obelisk that stands in front of the basilica's north entrance, flanked by two medieval bell towers. Both facades have loggias—balconies that can be used for solemn blessings.

Principal Façade

The main entrance to the Basilica faces the city walls and a large, empty square. At the end of the square, opposite the façade, across the busy street is the Monument to St. Francis of Assisi, built in 1927. The saint, who came to Rome as a pilgrim and met Pope Innocent III in the Lateran, who approved his rule for the little brothers, is represented in the company of his confreres. If viewing this monument from behind, the raised hands of St. Francis seem to sustain the basilica's façade. This effect was created by the artist of the monument, Giuseppe Tonnini, and it reminds the pilgrim of the legend, according to which Pope Innocent III, in a dream, saw St. Francis holding up the Lateran basilica. This monument, placed in front of the Pope's cathedral not only glorifies one of the most loved Italian saints, but also recalls that through the history of the Church many men and women were called by God "to restore his Church" by loving and self-giving service.

Nothing has survived from the ancient basilica's façade that had a large mosaic image of the Holy Savior. Alessandro Galilei designed the present façade in 1735 A.D. The colossal statues over the front remind the pilgrim of the entrance to St. Peters, which is mistakenly perceived by many believers as the principal church of Rome. Also here, as at St. Peters, over the main door is a statue of Jesus Christ, to whom this basilica was originally dedicated. St. John Baptist and St. John Evangelist, whose names are associated with the basilica now, flank Jesus; at the sides are statues of the doctors of the Latin and Greek Church, signifying the doctrinal unity of the Church of Christ. On each side of the central entrance is the inscription "The most Holy Church of the Lateran, Mother and Head of all the Churches of City and of the World."

The Principal Portico

The principal portico is also similar to the one of St. Peter's basilica. Five doors correspond to the five naves. At the left end of the Portico stands the marble statue of Constantine, the builder of the first basilica. This statue dates from Constantine's time, the 4th century, and was brought here from the Quirinal hill. The main door

Façade of Basilica of St. John Lateran and Statue of St. Francic of Assisi, Rome, Italy

Courtesy of New Diacolor, Rome

is probably from the 2nd century A.D. and is from the *Curia Hostilia* (the Senate) of the Roman Forum. It was transferred and installed here by Pope Alexander VII in 1660 A.D. The presence of this door in the principal church of Rome was meant to symbolize that the old authority of the ancient world is substituted by the rule of Christ. To the extreme right from the principal door is the Holy door.

Interior

The central nave of the ancient basilica was transformed into a Baroque hall by Francesco Borromini, who preserved the beautiful 15th century marble mosaic floor and the gorgeous ceiling of the 16th century, but changed the rows of columns separating the naves into rows of powerful pillars, which support arches. In the niches of the pillars are statues of the twelve apostles, who are "the pillars" or columns of the Church. These statues are of the school of Bernini. Beautiful columns of ancient green marble flank them.

The twelve bas-reliefs above the statues of apostles, designed by Alessandro Algardi and executed by Antonio Raggi, represent scenes of the Old and New Testaments in a so-called "Biblical Concordance," which shows the life of Jesus the Messiah prefigured in the Old Testament. The scenes of the Old Testament start at the entrance on the left wall and the scenes of the New Testament begin at the entrance on the right wall of the nave. Among the high windows are oval oil paintings, representing twelve prophets.

In this way the walls of the central nave represent the history of salvation—from the prophets, through Jesus the Messiah, to the Apostles, who founded the first ecclesial communities. And the Church of Rome has a special ministry to the unity of these ecclesial communities (Ephesians 2:19–22).

Floor

The rich marble mosaic floor, the work of the Cosmati family, renovated by Pope Martin V in 1425 A.D. at the end of Great Western schism, was created not only as decoration but also as an indication or guide for liturgical processions, so abundant in the liturgical tradition of Rome. The elaborated path of colorful marble figures leads to the altar. Through participation in liturgy, by following the pattern on the floor, the faithful enter into the story of salvation, the saving mysteries of the faith. In this way, the floor design itself shows the dynamic of salvation and the faithful's participation in it.

Pontifical Altar

In the front of the altar is the crypt, formed as a Confessio that contains, not the tomb of a martyr, but the tomb of Pope Martin V (+1433 A.D.), who wanted to have his ultimate resting place within this basilica. His election in Constance ended the Great Schism of the West. Pope Martin V restored the much damaged cathedral of Rome and chose to be buried here. The tomb is covered with a bronze lid, representing the Pope in liturgical vestments. The author of the lid is a Florentine artist, Giovanni Ghini.

For centuries, only the Pontiffs were allowed to celebrate Mass at the Pontifical altar, that enshrines the relic of the table, believed to be the altar of St. Peter from the house of Pudentius. Above the white marble altar, or *mensa,* rises the elegant, stately canopy, built in Gothic forms in 1367 A.D. by Giovanni da Stefano. Four columns support the reliquary, decorated with statues and paintings. The statues are images of the four evangel-

ists. The paintings by the famous medieval artist of Rome, Antoniazzo Romano, represent the scene of Crucifixion with Mary, St. John the Evangelist, St. Peter and St. Paul, St. John the Baptist, and other saints. Behind the gilded grill are the silver busts of St. Peter and St. Paul.

The Transept

The old transept of the basilica was reconstructed in 1601 A.D. by the pontifical architect Giacomo della Porta, who created the grandiose, luminous hall, that meets those who enter the basilica from the northern

Interior of Basilica of St. John Lateran
Courtesy of New Diacolor, Rome

230

portico. At the left aisle of the transept is the sumptuous Chapel of the Blessed Sacrament. The four columns of gilt bronze are from the Temple of Jupiter on the Capitoline hill and are installed here for the praise of the true God. Jasper and lapislazuli ornament the tabernacle. Over the tabernacle behind the bronze bas-relief representing the Last Supper is preserved a piece of the wooden table, which, according to an ancient tradition, was the table of the Last Supper. At the sides of the altar are statues of Moses and Elijah (at the right) and of Aaron and Melchisedek (at the left)—representing the Law, the Prophets, and the Priesthood of the Old Testament.

On the walls of the transept are paintings of the Roman Mannerist school of the late sixteenth and early seventeenth century which recount the story of the conversion of Constantine and of the building of the Lateran basilica. In the left wing of the transept is a monument over the tomb of the Pope Leo XIII, who contributed much to the restoring of the basilica in the last century. By the will of this Pope in 1885, the ancient deambulatory around the apse was dismantled in order to enlarge the space. The actual decoration of the lower part of the apse and solemn Episcopal throne is the work of the architect Francesco Vespigni, who chose to imitate the style of presbyteries of ancient Christian basilicas, and in such form to stress the antiquity and tradition of this place.

The Mosaic of the Apse

The prized mosaic of the apse is the result of two different time periods. The upper part with the dark blue background, which represents the bust of the

Savior among the clouds and surrounded by angels, as well as the very lower part, that depicts the river Jordan with tiny symbolical figures, is from late 4th century. The rest of the mosaic with the golden background is the work of the celebrated Franciscan Friar, Jacoppo Torriti, and his companion, Jacopo da Camerino. This work was commissioned by the Franciscan Pope Nicholas IV in 1292 A.D. and was finished shortly before the first Holy Year of 1300. While not intended directly for the Holy Year, this mosaic does represent a beautiful theological image of God's grace and of the mystery of Church.

In the center of the mosaic, right below the bust of the Savior, is a jeweled Cross. Between Christ and the Cross is the Dove of the Holy Spirit. From the Holy Spirit flows the water that showers the Cross and mingles with water streaming from the center of the Cross, where there is a small image of the baptism of Jesus. In such a way, the Cross symbolizes the fountain of baptismal water and reminds the pilgrim that through Baptism, the Christian enters into the dying and rising of Jesus. The stream of living water splits into the four rivers of paradise (Revelation 21), which also may be interpreted as the four books of the Gospels. The two deer, symbolizing the soul (Psalm 42), and the sheep, which symbolize believers, drink from the rivers. The waters of the rivers turn into the Jordan, filled by many scenes of daily human life and thus signify that the salvation of the Lord encompasses all of human temporal reality.

Between the four rivers stands Celestial Jerusalem, the ideal image of the Church (Hebrews 12:22). In the center of

Celestial Jerusalem grows the palm that is the tree of eternal life. On the branch of this palm tree sits the Phoenix bird, an ancient symbol of the Resurrection. The apostles St. Peter and St. Paul are standing at the sides of the tree. The celestial Jerusalem-Paradise is surrounded by a wall and guarded by an angel bearing a sword (Genesis 3:24).

The mosaic moves the pilgrim to consider the mystery of Baptism as a sacrament that with the Eucharist forms the very base of the Church. Baptism, although received only once, continues to unfold in the life of the believer. As one journeys in the Christian life, the graces of Baptism flow ever deeper into the mind and heart, fostering a closer relation-ship to Jesus and a greater participation in his mission. This truth is emphasized by the figures of saints, that are flanking the cross/baptismal font.

Apse mosaic of Basilica of
St. John Lateran, Rome
Courtesy of author Dr. Irena Vaisvilaite

At the sides of the Cross stand Mary and St. John Baptist. Behind Mary kneels the small figure of Pope Nicholas IV. Between him and the figures of St. Peter and St. Paul is an image of St. Francis, smaller in size than the two apostles. Behind St. John the Baptist stands another smaller figure in a Franciscan habit, St. Anthony, followed by larger figures of St. John Evangelist and St. Andrew, the brother of St. Peter. The presence of the two almost contemporary Franciscan saints is due to Pope Nicholas IV, who was a Franciscan himself, but also indicates the importance that St. Francis and St. Anthony gained in the Western Church by the end of the thirteenth century.

Before leaving the Lateran basilica, the pilgrim might wish to visit the medieval Courtyard, constructed in the years 1215–1223 A.D. by Pietro Vassaletto and his son. The courtyard closely resembles another work of these artists, the courtyard of St. Paul's Outside the Walls, and likewise represents the island of peace. On the walls are exposed fragments from the old basilica. In the center of the courtyard stands a beautiful work of the Carolingian period (8th century), acclaimed by popular tradition as the "Well of the Samaritan woman."

Leaving Basilica

When exiting the basilica from the principal entrance, it is possible to see the fragment of the Giotto fresco, representing Boniface VIII proclaiming the Holy Year 1300. This fragment was rescued from the old basilica and now is enshrined at the end of the first left nave, when looking from the altar.

If leaving the basilica from the Northern portico, through the double porch, built by Domenco Fontana, the pilgrim will exit into a solemn square with the highest obelisk in Rome in it center. This obelisk, dating from 1500 B.C., was brought to Rome in 357 A.D. and installed into the Circus Maximus. In 1588 A.D. Pope Sixtus V, preparing Rome for the Jubilee of 1600 A.D., ordered a marking of the most important Christian monuments by obelisks, taken from ancient sites. The obelisk of the Lateran basilica is clearly visible from the via Merulana, a street constructed by Pope Sixtus V for the purpose of enabling the pilgrims to reach the Lateran, when going from the Esquiline hill or coming from the Basilica of the Holy Cross, *(Santa Croce)*, which is situated not far from the porta S. Giovanni, next to the city walls.

The square at the end of four streets is formed by the loggia of benedictions of the basilica's façade and by the new Lateran palace, built in 1595 A.D. There is almost nothing now that remains from the old bishop's palace. In 1592 A.D., the old palace was destroyed by the will of Pope Sixtus V, who wanted to construct this new and modern building. This palace was never was used as the popes' residence. Through the centuries, it had different functions and now it is the palace of the Chancery of the Diocese of Rome and the Museum of Pontifical history, rarely open for visitors.

Baptistery

At the right side of the square, when facing the loggia, is the very important Baptistery of the Lateran. This Baptistery in the

Lateran was built in the fourth century, in the time of Constantine, who, according to the *Liber Pontificalis,* gave to the Baptistery many sumptuous gifts. Legend insists that Constantine was baptized here. This is historically inaccurate because Constantine, although recognizing Christianity as one of the legitimate religions of the Roman Empire, and later giving to the Church extensive privileges, was baptized himself only on his deathbed and perhaps never even saw the Baptistery completed.

The building was reconstructed in the fifth century by the will of Pope Sixtus III and in 1637 A.D. by Pope Urbanus VIII, who ordered the reconstruction of the entrance to the Baptistery. On the opposite side of the building is the ancient, solemn entrance flanked by porphyry columns which still has some of the original rich marble decorations, indicating the imperial origin of this building.

Due to the respect for the Baptistery already in early times, from the 5th to the 11th centuries, four oratories and chapels were built around the central space. In the center of the building is the Baptismal font. Originally the font was designed for baptism by immersion. Now in the center of this font stands a smaller one, made from marble at the end of the fourteenth century. The *Liber Pontificalis* contains a description of the ancient appearance of the baptismal font. Water to the font came by aqueduct and poured into the basin from seven silver statues of deer and one golden statue of a Lamb. The octangular basin inside was covered by silver. In the center of the basin there was a column of porphyry that had on the top a golden ampoule with oil. On the opposite sides of the basin were statues of Jesus and St. John the Baptist, also made from silver. The catechumen of the ancient Church, when entering the font for Baptism by immersion, would enter from the side of St. John Baptist, and exit at the side of the statue of Jesus. In this way, the ritual symbolized dying and rising in Jesus, and passing from the old way of life into the new.

On the walls of the dome and of the central hall of the Baptistery are frescoes, painted by Andrea Sacchi and other artists of 17th century. These frescoes represent the life of St. John Baptist and of the Emperor Constantine. Two tiers of columns surmount the large font, which in later times was given a circular form. The lower ones are from porphyry and the upper ones from white marble. The building of the Baptistery is still octagonal and the number of columns, surrounding the basin, is eight. The number eight has an eschatological meaning, indicating the "eighth day" of the week, a new time, eternity. God's time, *kairos*, takes the place of ordinary time, *chronos*.

Reflection

This beautiful Baptistery of the Lateran basilica, the womb of the mother church of Rome, where Christian converts were reborn in the waters of new life, invites the pilgrim to a renewal of the baptismal commitment to live the Christ mystery. Living out one's baptism means seeking Christ in the joys and sorrows, the hopes and fears of each day, realizing that this pattern of life is a sharing in the mystery of the dying and rising of the Lord (Romans 6:3–11).

Prayerful reflection in this holy place might be fostered by meditating on the inscription, carved on the cornice of columns above the baptismal font. Pope Sixtus III composed this inscription around 435 A.D. It reads:

> *The brood born here to live in heaven has life from water and the fructifying spirit. Sinner, seek your cleansing in this stream that takes the old and gives a new person back. No barrier can divide where life unites: one faith, one fount, one Spirit make one people. A Virgin still, the Church gives birth to children conceived of God, delivered in the water. Washed in this bath the stains will float away that mark the guilt of Adam and your own. The stream that flows below sprang from the wounded Christ to wash the whole world clean and give it life. Children of the water, think no more of earth; heaven will give you joy; in heaven hope. Think not your sins too many or too great: birth in this stream is birth to holiness.*

Also connected to the Lateran complex of buildings is the former chapel of the Popes, the so-called Sancta Sanctorum, the "holy of holies," named after the innermost sanctuary of Solomon's Temple in ancient Jerusalem (1 Kings 6–8). This chapel is located at the top of the so-called Holy Stairs, the Scala Santa, which tradition says were transported back from the Holy Land by Helena, the mother of Emperor Constantine. It was believed that these were the stairs from the Palace of Pilate and were used by Jesus himself during the process of his trial on Good Friday. The stairs were actually in the old pontifical Lateran palace and were brought here by Pope Sixtus V after the demolishment of the old palace. Pilgrims climb these stairs, composed of twenty-eight steps, on their knees as an act of devotion to the Passion of Jesus. Upon reaching the top of the stairs, it is possible to look into the Sancta Sanctorum from a window and view the altar and image of the Savior which hangs over it. There are two modern staircases on either side of the holy stairs, which allow the pilgrim to descend or to reach the upper level of the building that holds the Sancta Sanctorum.

Holy Stairs,
Scala Sancta, Rome

Courtesy of author Dr. Irena Vaisvilaite

It was here in this private papal chapel that the most important relics of Rome were kept. The existence of the chapel is documented from the 5th century. At that time it was dedicated to St. Lawrence, a Roman deacon and martyr. The relics of the Roman martyrs, St. Peter and St. Paul, St. Lawrence and St. Agnes, as well as the first Christian martyr, St. Stephen, were kept here. Later various objects, believed to be the relics of the Passion of the Lord, were transferred here. But the name of the Sancta Sanctorum, "the Holy of Holies," was related to the image called the Acheropita, the sacred image of

239

Jesus, an icon "made not by human hands," present in Rome from the end of the 6th century. This icon was considered to be a miraculous image of Jesus, which was imprinted by the Lord himself on a piece of cloth. This image was included into a larger image, painted on a board. Some scholars believe that the Acheropita from the Sancta Sanctorum later became known as the Veil of Veronica, shown to the pilgrims from the year 1200A A.D. and later during the Jubilee years. The emotional reaction of pilgrims, when seeing this relic in 1300 A.D., was expressed by Dante in the Divine Comedy:

> *Like a man who perhaps from Crotia comes to*
> *see our Veronica,*
> *And while it is shown, stares at it with never-sated-gaze,*
> *And with his old hungry longing thinks to himself,*
> *"My Lord Jesus Christ, true God, didst Thou who I see,*
> *So look, was this then Thy true semblance?"*

(Paradiso, XXXI)

Fifty years later during the Jubilee of 1350 A.D., another great Italian poet, Petrarch, gave witness to this devotion to the Holy Face:

> *The little old white-haired man prepares to leave,*
> *The sweet place that has watched him grow old,*
> *And from that family filled with fear,*
> *Who sees their dear father leave,*
> *Then dragging his ancient limbs hither,*

To follow the object of his yearning,
And comes to Rome,
To gaze at the likeness of Him,
Whom he hopes to see again in heaven.

(Sonnet XVI)

Pope Nicholas III renovated this chapel in 1277–1280 A.D. From this renovation dates the beautiful frescoes and mosaic decoration, featuring the scenes of martyrdom of the above-mentioned saints, and of Pope Nicholas III, who, along with St. Peter and St. Paul, offer the chapel to Christ. The chapel's interior is embellished by porphyry columns and a cosmatesque floor. The inscription above the altar is from Pope Sixtus V and states: *Non est toto sanctior orbe locus* (There is no holier place in the world than this).

Reflection

The Sancta Sanctorum expresses the inner desire of the pilgrim to encounter God in an intimate way, indeed, face to face. Moses could not look upon the face of God, but now, through the Incarnation, Jesus has revealed the image of the Father (Hebrews 1:1–3). Christ is the image of the invisible God. This chapel of the holy of holies challenges the pilgrim to seek God's face in people and situations which perhaps seem unlikely. In a particular way, Jesus urges the Christian to seek his face in the hungry, the thirsty, the naked, the prisoner, the sick, and the marginalized (Matthew 25:31–46).

Basilica of St. Mary Major

Liturgical Feast Days Associated with the Basilica—Solemnity of the Mother of God, January 1, The Annunciation, March 25, the Dedication of St. Mary Major (Our Lady of the Snows), August 5, Christmas, December 25.

The Basilica of St. Mary Major calls the pilgrim to consider the figure of Mary, Mother of God and Mother of the Church. Built in the 5th century, in honor of the title "Mother of God," conferred on Mary at the Council of Ephesus in 431 A.D., this church is a testimony to the essential role of Mary in God's plan of salvation history. By saying "yes" to the angel Gabriel at the Annunciation (Luke 1:26–38), Mary opened herself to God and his sovereign will by agreeing to be the mother of the Messiah. Mary gives birth to the Word-made-flesh and offers him to the world for the sake of its salvation (TMA 2). In this way, she becomes a model for all believers who are called to give birth to the Word in their own lives, making his healing and life-giving power present in all times and places.

History

According to the medieval legend, the first church dedicated to Mary was on the Esquiline hill, built by Pope Liberius (352–366 A.D.) on the site of an ancient market place. Legend states that on the vigil of August 5, the Virgin Mary appeared in a dream to the Pope and to a Roman patrician, John, and told them that she wanted a church built in her honor on the site where the snow would fall that night. The next morning, there was snow upon the Esquiline hill. The Pope drew the outline of the church in the snow. Since then the feast of our "Lady of the Snows" is celebrated on August 5. During the Mass on this feast, a snowfall of white rose petals descends from the ceiling of the church, to commemorate the miracle.

According to tradition, the original edifice of Liberius was demolished one hundred years later, immediately after the Council of Ephesus (431 A.D.), and a much larger basilica, dedicated to the "Mother of God," was built by Pope Sixtus III (432–440 A.D.). Archeologists are able to find only this one building, though, and no remains of previous Christian buildings. This 5th-century basilica was given the title of Mother of God, bestowed on Mary by the Council of Ephesus. As all the great basilicas of Rome, this one was also rebuilt and restored many times and preserves traces of different centuries. Great artists such as Giotto, Pietro Cavallini, Arnolfo di Cambio, Jacopo Torriti, and Pietro della Francesca worked here, but not all of their works have survived. The modern Baroque appearance is due to the work of three famous architects of the 18th century, Carlo Rainaldi, Flaminio Ponzio and Ferdinando Fuga. They created an elegant container for the body of the ancient basilica.

Since medieval times Romans have believed that the relics of the Manger of Bethlehem or even the whole Grotto itself was transferred into the Basilica of St. Mary Major. For these relics the Oratory of the Crib, the Oratorium ad Presepe was built. Since ancient times, on Christmas morning, a procession of the Santa

Culla, the Holy Crib, is held in the basilica. Saint Ignatius of Loyola celebrated his first Mass in this oratory. The image of Mary with the Child known as the *Salus Populi Romani,* the salvation of the Roman people, is in the Borghese chapel. Romans have an exceptional devotion for this image.

Approaching St. Mary's Basilica

The Basilica of St. Mary Major is built on the edge of a hill and therefore has two entries, one from the central façade and one from the side of the apse. On both sides of the basilica are large piazzas or squares. The apsidal façade is approached by an imposing flight of steps from the Piazza Esquilino. In front of the majestic, beautifully curved apse stands an obelisk, indicating to pilgrims the importance of this church.

Exterior of Basilica of St. Mary Major, Rome

Courtesy of author Dr. Irena Vaisvilaite

244

In the middle of the busy Piazza Santa Maria Maggiore stands a column of beautiful marble, *cipollino*, from the basilica of Maxentius in the Roman forum. This column, crowned by a statue of the Virgin Mary, was put here by the will of Pope Paul V in 1613 A.D. From this square, the pilgrim might admire the campanille or bell tower (built in 1377 A.D.), which is the highest in Rome, and the elegant late Baroque façade created by Ferdinando Fuga in 1743 A.D. Behind the loggia, some mosaics of the old basilica are visible. These mosaics were created during the pontificate of Pope Nicholas IV (1294–1308 A.D.). They depict Christ Panocrator sitting in glory upon a heavenly throne, as well as the story of the miracle of the snow of Pope Liberius. These mosaics can be better viewed from the loggia, which can be accessed from the portico of the basilica. From this loggia is a good view of the basilica of St. John Lateran, which is situated at the end of the via Merulana. Through the centuries on Easter morning, the image of Mary from the Basilica of Saint Mary Major, the *Salus Populi Romani*, and the image of the Acheropitos, from the Sancta Sanctorum, were carried in processions that met halfway between the two basilicas.

Interior

The basilica's interior is vast and well proportioned. It still preserves the ancient basilican form and is enriched by testimonies of Marian devotion through the centuries. The space is divided into three naves by two rows of beautiful columns. Over the capitals of the columns runs a mosaic frieze with a grapevine on a golden background. The richly ornate marble floor is the work of the Cosmati family. The wooden ceiling is decorated by gold brought from America by Christopher Columbus and presented to Pope Alexander VI by the Spanish King Ferdinand and Queen Isabella.

The walls of the central nave and the triumphal arch at the end of this nave are decorated with mosaics from the time of Sixtus III (432–440 A.D.). "Bishop Sixtus for the People of God" states the dedicatory inscription upon the arch. In his times, the basilica was flooded with light, since the widows of the central nave were placed very near to each other. Since then, every second one is bricked up, which makes it difficult to view the beautiful mosaics that are immediately below the windows. This oldest mosaic cycle in Rome depicts salvation history through the lives of Abraham and Jacob (on the left-hand side from the entrance) and of Moses and Joshua (on the right hand side).

Interior of Basilica of St. Mary Major, Rome

Courtesy of Basilica di Santa Maria Maggiore, Rome, Italy

This salvation history cycle is completed by the scenes of the Incarnation and the infancy of Christ on the triumphal arch. On the top of the arch, in the center, is a jewel-studded throne with an upright Cross. Below, starting on the upper left, the Annunciation is represented. This early image offers quite an elaborate theology. Both Mary and Joseph are present in the scene. Mary dressed as a princess, which indicates her choseness, sits in front of her locked house, which is a symbol of her virginity. The House of Joseph, who was believed to be widower, is opened. Not one but six angels, messengers of God, are surrounding Mary and Joseph. It is interesting that there is no Nativity scene. In fifth century, when these mosaics were created, the artistic representation of the Nativity was not yet that wide-spread. Instead, there is the scene of Epiphany or Adoration of the Magi (Matthew 2:1–12), which is in the middle level. The three Magi stand before the throne of the Infant Jesus, who is dressed as an adult philosopher, and therefore represents Divine Wisdom. Mary is sitting on the left of the throne. On the right side of the throne sits Rachel, the mother of Israel, who weeps for her children. At the lowest level is depicted the massacre of the infants of Bethlehem (Matthew 2:16–18). At the foot of arch is an image of Jerusalem with six sheep, which symbolize faithful Christians of Jewish decent gathering at the gate.

The images on the right side of arch continue the salvation story. On the top level is the scene of the Presentation in the Temple (Luke 2:21–40), on the middle is the Flight into Egypt (Matthew 2:13–15) and on the lowest level is depicted the Magi before Herod. At the foot of arch is an image of

Bethlehem. The six sheep, which gather at the gate of Bethlehem, symbolize Christians of Gentile descent. Together with the other six lambs standing at the gate of Jerusalem, they represent the whole Church, the new Israel, the flock of God (John 10:16).

The apse mosaics are not as old as the ones of the central nave and of the triumphal arch. They were created during the pontificate of Pope Nicholas IV (1288–1292 A.D.), who tore down the earlier apse and replaced it with a larger one. This apse is decorated with stories of Mary's life that are below the central scene of the Coronation of the Virgin. The scenes of Mary's life repeat, in part, the ones on the triumphal arch—from the left to the right are the Annunciation, the Nativity, the Dormition, the Adoration of the Magi, and the Presentation. The most important one of this cycle is in the center. The Dormition, or the *Transitus*, is the traditional representation of the firm belief that Mary, after her earthly life, is now with her Son. This tradition is common to both the Eastern and the Western Church. The composition shows Mary laid out on her deathbed surrounded with the mourning apostles and angels. In the center stands Christ in an almond-shaped nimbus known as a mandorla. The mandorla is a symbol of the new, eternal life in Glory. Jesus is taking his Mother into this life. In his arms he holds a small figure of an old woman wrapped in a funeral shroud. This image expresses the same theological "locus" that the much later (1950) dogma of Assumption of Mary taught. The image shows that Mary did not "ascend" into heaven but was carried by her Son, who is her Savior and the Savior of the whole human race.

The central Apse mosaic represents her being crowned by Christ and sitting on the same throne with him. But Mary is not the center of action, nor does she take any initiative. The difference between things human and things divine is carefully maintained in this artwork, while reflecting the high Mariology of the medieval age. Dominating in the composition are the figures of Jesus and Mary in the circle filled with stars and surrounded by angelic choirs. The sun and the moon are under the feet of the Son and the Mother. Both are seated on the same cushioned and jeweled throne. Jesus with one hand places the crown on Mary's head and in the other he holds the book with the inscription: "Come, my chosen one, and I will place you on my throne."

The upper space of the apse is filled with spirals of branches of the trees of Paradise. Peacocks and phoenixes, which are symbols of the Resurrection and eternal life, are perching on the branches. From the left side of the scene of the Coronation are represented the figures of St. Francis of Assisi, St. Peter, and St. Paul. The smaller figure of the kneeling Pope is an image of Pope Nicholas IV, who commissioned this mosaic. From the left side of the central image kneels another small figure in clerical vestments. This is Cardinal Giacomo Colonna, who shared the expenses of the mosaic with the Pope. Also depicted are St. John Baptist, St. John Evangelist and St. Anthony of Padua. The apse mosaic was created by the Franciscan Jacopo Torriti, who also worked on the apse in the basilica of St. John in Lateran. The mosaics in both apses were commissioned by the same Nicholas IV, who was a Franciscan himself, and who wanted to include two recently canonized Franciscan saints into his artwork. Therefore, St. Francis and St. Anthony are incorporated into the mosaics of two great basilicas.

Apse Mosaic, Basilica of St. Mary Major, Rome

Courtesy of Basilica di Santa Maria Maggiore, Rome, Italy

At the base of the entire composition of the mosaic runs a river filled with river birds and fish. The signature of the artist Jacopo Torriti is at the extreme left. On the top of the composition, outside of the apse's arch, is an enthroned Lamb. At his sides are symbols of the four evangelists and the twenty-four elders from the book of Revelation. Beneath these are two more scenes. On the left is St. Jerome explaining the Scriptures to Paola and Eustochia, and on the right is St. Matthew preaching to the Hebrews. Both scenes are related to the relics of Matthew and Jerome, brought to this basilica from the East and placed in the central altar.

Reflection

In the mosaic cycle of St. Mary Major, the entire history of salvation is represented, from the Old Testament to the eschatological future of bodily resurrection. These biblical scenes not only unfold the plan of God's salvation in human history, but they also inspire the pilgrim to consider how these events impact and inform the life of every believer. The Lord of history, who reveals himself in time and space, invites the pilgrim to enter into the story, his story, the story of salvation. In this way, God's story becomes one's own story and the biblical events take on a whole new meaning. No longer are these scenes simply the subject of nostalgia, or a trip down memory lane for the people of God. Rather they become opportunities for the pilgrim to enter more profoundly into the dynamic of God's constant desire to save, heal, liberate, and redeem his people. Each mosaic panel can be a window into the pilgrim's own relationship with the God of the story.

The main altar has a porphyry ciborium by Fredinando Fuga, who used the columns of the earlier, 15th century ciborium. The urn of porphyry with gilded ornaments, placed beneath the altar, holds relics of St. Matthew. In the front of the altar is the Confessio, which holds the relics of Christ's Manger. These relics are believed to have been brought from Bethlehem at the same time as the body of St. Jerome. The crystal and silver reliquary was designed by the famous classical artist, Valadier. In front of the niche with the reliquary is a statue of Pope Pius IX, kneeling in prayer, which was created by Ignazio Iacometti.

At the right side of the altar, at the step is the simple slab of the tomb of the great Baroque artist, Gian Lorenzo Bernini. The inscription reads: "Gian Lorenzo Bernini, who brought honor to art and to the city here humbly lies." The artist's father, Pietro Bernini, who worked for the Borghese or Paoline chapel in this basilica, is also buried here.

The chapel to the right of the altar is called the Sixtine chapel after Pope Sixtus V, who began the reconstruction of this chapel while he was still a cardinal. The architect of the chapel was Domenico Fontana, who was told by the Pope that the Manger of Bethlehem would be transported here. These are the prized relics of this basilica. This Oratory, which Romans believed contained the Grotto of Bethlehem and the relics of the Manger, is now located in the confessio under the main altar of the chapel, which was built in 1289 A.D. by Arnolfo di Cambio. He created the famous Nativity scene that is now in the confessio of the Sixtine chapel and can be visited only during the Christmas season. Because of the relics of the Manger, Santa Maria Maggiore is the only church in Rome that does not feature a Presepe, a Nativity scene or Creche, during Christmas.

9th century A.D. Byzantine icon entitled: Salus Populi Romani, from the Pauline Chapel, Basilica of St. Mary Major, Rome

Courtesy of Basilica di Santa Maria Maggiore, Roma

The Altar in the chapel's center has a very beautiful ciborium. Four gilded bronze statues of angels hold the tempietto, the small building similar to a chapel. Against the walls of the chapel are the tombs of Pope Sixtus V (1588–1589 A.D.) and Saint Pius V (1566–1572 A.D.).

At the left side from the main altar is the so-called Pauline chapel or Borghese chapel, commissioned to Falminio Ponzio by Pope Paul V (1605–1621 A.D.) from the Borghese family. This Pope built the chapel for the most venerated image of Virgin Mary, the *Salus populi Romani*. This icon of the Byzantine style is from the ninth century, but pious Medieval Romans believed it was painted by the evangelist St. Luke. The icon is over the central altar of the chapel and is handsomely framed and surrounded by five guilded bronze statues of angels. Mary is represented holding Jesus, who is dressed in a golden tunic and holds the book. The hands of Mary are crossed in front of her child. One hand exposes two fingers, which is a sign of the two natures of the person of Christ, who is both human and divine. This image was placed in the chapel on January 27, 1613. At the same time, the column with the statue of Mary was erected in front of the basilica's main entrance.

The relief above the altar is by Stefano Maderno. It depicts Pope Liberius marking the dimensions of the basilica in the snow. The tombs of Popes Paul V and his predecessor Pope Clement VIII (1592–1605 A.D.) are in this chapel. Pope Pius XII, who, as many Romans, had a special devotion to the image of the Salus Populi Romani, celebrated his first Mass here. During the years of the persecution of the Church under the communist regime in the former Soviet Union, prayer services for the so-called "Church of Silence" used to take place in this chapel regularly.

Before leaving the basilica, the pilgrim might take time in the Sixtine or the Pauline chapels, which are reserved for prayer. Daily masses are celebrated in the Pauline chapel.

Reflection

Although not built on the site of a tomb of a martyr or a saint, the basilica of Mary Major has in its crypt beneath the altar, according to tradition, relics of the crib of the infant Jesus from Bethlehem. This draws the mind of the pilgrim to the mystery of the Incarnation, God becoming human so that humans might become godlike. Mary's role in the Incarnation demonstrates how God allows human free will to be part of the dialogue of salvation. Her decision to say yes at the Annunciation came only after she asked: "How can this be?" (Luke 1:26–38) The Christian vocation is a free response to the God who beckons, invites, and draws the human heart into a dialogue of love.

This conversation of conversion is revealed in the life of Mary, who treasured all things in her heart (Luke 2:19). The pilgrim to this basilica is challenged by the example of Mary to ponder the unfolding events of life and, through prayer, come to see these daily events as opportunities to experience fully the good news of salvation (TMA 43, 48, 54). Mary's *yes* had to keep expanding throughout her life, as she embraced relationships and situations that she could have never anticipated back on the day of her encounter with the angel Gabriel. And ultimately that freely uttered *yes* had to expand far enough to allow her the courage to stand at the foot of her own Son's Cross. Mary shows the pilgrim how the "yes of faith" must be repeated through triumphs and defeats, pleasures and pain, so as to pass through death into resurrection.

Conclusion

The pilgrimage to Rome is the foundation of the Jubilee traditions. Journeying to the threshold of the Apostles, *ad limina apostolorum*, was the basis for the development of many other Jubilee traditions and ceremonies. The pilgrim who goes to Rome for the Jubilee 2000 will encounter the working of God's grace through signs and symbols, liturgies and processions. In this way, the pilgrim experiences Jesus, the Word made flesh, through the tangible sights and sounds of the Roman sojourn. This incarnational spirituality is complemented by the mystical dimension of the "great cloud of witnesses" which surround the pilgrim—the Apostles, Martyrs, and Saints of Rome. The veneration of devotional images and relics, the Holy Door rituals, the four basilica pilgrimage, and the obtaining of the Jubilee indulgence are all ways of encountering Jesus, who is the Jubilee.

CONCLUSION

BACK TO THE BEGINNING

Returning to the Source

A pilgrimage is not just a journey. It also involves the encounter of pilgrims with rituals, holy objects, and sacred architecture, as outlined in this book. In addition, pilgrimage is as much about returning home as it is about the process itself. The souvenirs, photographs, and stories of the adventure, which are brought home by the pilgrim, form a type of spiritual recollection and help to reconstruct the sacred journey in the imagination. Once home, these tangible objects of pilgrimage provide an imaginative link with the sacred goal or destination of the pilgrimage. Returning back, the pilgrim can share the sacred geography of the journey with those who have stayed at home and who await some blessing from the returning traveler.

257

The pilgrim's instinct is deeply set in the human heart. So, even those who have stayed home can relate to the stories of pilgrimage, since they too aspire to make their own journey in the future. A pilgrimage is a form of retreat, focusing the mind and heart on God in the physical act of the traversing of distance. At the same time, pilgrimage can also be a form of witness, an outward sign to others of faith. Those who are exposed to the witness of the pilgrim can be challenged to a rededication of faith in their own lives. The pilgrim's experience and stories becomes part of the living tradition of worship and community. This witness becomes part of the stream of the living tradition of believers down through the centuries, who have visited and worshiped at these sacred sites, and then returned home to share their blessings.

From Pilgrim to Witness

The returning to the source, the arrival home, is the temporal end of the adventure. But in a deeper spiritual sense, the experience continues as the pilgrim attempts to integrate the lessons, insights, and graces of the journey into daily life. Once the religious duty of the pilgrimage is fulfilled, and the religious desire, which impelled the pilgrim to make the trip, is satisfied then the integration of this mystical adventure must begin. In a way, the pilgrim has acquired a new wisdom, which must be offered as a gift to the community which receives the pilgrim back.

Part of the witness of the returning pilgrim is that the entire people of God is on a journey to the heavenly city. "For here we have no lasting city, but we seek the one that is to come" (Hebrews 13:14). The journey is a symbol of the spiritual quest of every Christian, who has no permanent place on earth (1 Peter 2:11). The witness of pilgrimage is an image of the heart's desire to approach God in trust and abandonment.

As presented in this book, the pilgrim encounters the workings of God's grace through signs and symbols, liturgies and processions, tangible sights and sounds. This incarnational spirituality, in which all of the human senses are filled with impressions and experiences, continues to unfold as the stories, souvenirs, and photographs are shared with others upon arrival home.

In Luke 24, after the two unnamed disciples encountered the risen Jesus on the road to Emmaus, they quickly returned to Jerusalem to tell others of their experience. "Then they recounted what had happened on the road and how they had come to know him in the breaking of bread" (Luke 24:35). Those who had witnessed the Resurrection now share with others their insights to lead them to their own encounter with the Lord. This gospel narrative of Luke confirms that pilgrims are transformed into witnesses by testifying to their experience of the road.

Holy Land Pilgrimage

The "fifth gospel" of the Holy Land is a physical, tangible witness to the events of the birth, life, death, and resurrection of Jesus. Salvation history is etched in the very rock, soil, and water of this land. Since the earliest times of Christianity, pilgrimage to the Holy Land has been a way of encountering the Lord through a "spirituality of place." The place where eternity had once entered into time has been the pilgrimage destination for those who have sought a tangible experience of the mysteries of salvation. Because of the Incarnation, Christian memory is inescapably bound to place.

The three major faiths of western civilization regard the Holy Land as sacred geography. For the Jew, it is the land of the Torah. For the Muslim, it is Abraham's country. And for the Christian, it is the land of both the Old and New Testaments. In a variety of ways, all of these religions have encountered God in the sanctified sites of this land.

Rome Pilgrimage

All roads lead to Rome, the eternal city. As the *caput mundi,* the head of the world, Rome has greatly influenced the history, language, culture, politics, religion, and fine arts of the western world. Known to Christians as the city of Apostles, Martyrs, and Saints, Rome became the destination for pilgrimage as early as the second century A.D.

The tombs of the Apostles, St. Peter and St. Paul, are the "trophies" marking the spiritual victory of these two founders of the Roman Church. Rome is the "new Jerusalem" of the Christian world and a center of apostolic teaching, tradition, and spirituality. Pilgrimage to the threshold of the Apostles, *ad limina apostolorum,* is a tangible form of veneration to the two founders of the "new Jerusalem." Rome has had a theological primacy among the various Sees of the Church since ancient times, because of the apostolic deposit of teaching, witness, and shed blood of St. Peter and St. Paul.

The wealth of this deposit of faith is made present and accessible to the pilgrim who journeys through the streets, squares, churches, and catacombs of Rome in search of deeper faith, hope, charity, and conversion of life. Besides the tombs of the apostles, there are many tombs and shrines of other Christian martyrs in Rome, dating from the first few centuries of Christianity. These tombs have always been considered to be places where heaven and earth meet.

The early Christians associated two spiritual realities with the tombs or shrines of the martyrs and saints—power and presence. According to this spirituality, the saint or martyr is not only present spiritually at the tomb, but also in the community that gathers to worship there. The power of the Saint or Martyr is to strengthen, heal, and edify the pilgrim, through their heavenly intercession. Christian pilgrims have long come to these sacred sites of Rome seeking physical, emotional, psychological, and spiritual healing through the powerful intercession of these heroes of faith.

Dynamic Integration of the Holy Land and Rome

In the minds and hearts of early Christian pilgrims, the Holy Land and the city of Rome became integrated and spiritually unified. Jerusalem was the site of the Passion, Death, and resurrection of Jesus, the sacred site of salvation. When Rome became the spiritual capital of Christianity after the martyrdoms of St. Peter and St. Paul, it was perceived as the "new Jerusalem," a "city set on a hill."

Jerusalem is a symbol of salvation. This city becomes an eschatological symbol as the heavenly Jerusalem, bedecked as a bride, descending from Heaven in the vision of John in Revelation 21:2. The city, as an archetype of the fullness of salvation, has a throne in the center on which is seated Jesus, as the alpha and omega, the King of the ages.

This dynamic integration of the symbols of Rome and the Holy Land is dramatically depicted in an ancient Christian mosaic from the 4th century A.D. in Rome. This apse mosaic of the Basilica of Saint Pudenziana in Rome harmonizes the city of Rome, as the center of the Church, with the Holy Land, as the sacred geography of salvation. In this mosaic, the risen Jesus is enthroned in glory, surrounded by the Apostles, who represent the foundation of the Church. In the background is the architecture of Jerusalem and Bethlehem of the 4th century A.D.

On one level of meaning, Jesus is depicted as a

4th century A.D. apse mosaic,
Basilica of St. Pudenziana, Rome

Courtesy of Basilica di Santa Pudenziana, Rome

teacher or philosopher, surrounded by his school of disciples. He is the new Moses, commissioning his Apostles to teach all nations the truth of his Gospel (Matthew 28:16–20). On another level, Jesus is the risen and exalted Lord, enthroned as the apocalyptic judge of the living and the dead (Matthew 25:31–32). He is flanked by the Twelve Apostles who will also sit on thrones of judgement on the last day. "In my kingdom you will eat and drink at my table, and you will sit on thrones judging the twelve tribes of Israel" (Luke 22:30). The college of apostles appears to suggest intense continuity with Israel and the Twelve Tribes. The Twelve Apostles in the Gospels link the Church to Israel (Matthew 19:28). On a third level of meaning, in a liturgical reading of this apse mosaic, this motif is a mirror image of the bishop seated on his cathedra surrounded by the presbyters. This scene would have been actualized below in the apse during the ancient liturgies in the basilica.

The college of Apostles in the mosaic depicts the apostolic teaching and witness as the foundation for the Church. The two dimensions of the Church in ancient times, the Church of the Gentiles and the Church of the Circumcised, are personified by the two allegorical female figures who are crowning St. Paul and St. Peter with the laurels of martyrdom. The ecclesia, or Church, is often symbolized in ancient Christian art as a female figure, usually praying. St. Paul, the great apostle to the Gentiles, is crowned by a woman dressed as a Gentile Roman matron. St. Peter, the apostle to the Jews, is crowned by a woman dressed as a Jewish matron. St. Paul and St. Peter flank Christ as the founders of the Roman Church, which was a mixed community of both Gentile and Jewish Christians. These two apostles are the new "Castor and Pollux" or "Romulus and Remus," joint founders of Church of Rome through their martyrdoms.

The teaching and testimony of the Apostles is preserved in the four Gospels of the New Testament. In the vault of Heaven of the mosaic are the four heavenly beasts, which symbolize the four Evangelists. Matthew is symbolized by the man, Mark by the lion, Luke by the ox, and John by the eagle. These living creatures are found in the visions of the Hebrew prophets Daniel and Ezekiel. In the New Testament, these beasts are apocalyptic symbols, which surround the throne of God, engaging in heavenly eternal worship. "Day and night, without pause, they sing: Holy, holy, holy is the Lord God Almighty, He who was, and who is, and who is to come!" (Revelation 4:6–8)

In the center of the mosaic, behind Jesus, is the Cross, surmounted on the hill of Golgotha. It is central to the mosaic because the Cross is central for salvation. The Cross is jeweled, highlighting the victory and precious nature of this symbol of redemption. It is not the agony and suffering of Jesus that is portrayed, rather it is the glory of the triumph of the crucified Jesus that is depicted. In a sense, the Cross is the throne of Christ. Both are jeweled, and they seem to be almost connected in the scene. The Messiah is enthroned on the Cross and reigns as a King in the Gospel of John.

The themes of the victory of the Cross and the role of Christ as both King and Judge are synthesized in the Preface for the Eucharistic Prayer for the Passion of the Lord, which states, in part:

The suffering and death of your Son brought life to the whole world, moving our hearts to praise your glory. The power of the cross reveals your judgement on this world and the kingship of Christ crucified.

The background of the mosaic is filled with an architectural skyline. Bethlehem and Jerusalem are depicted by the two basilicas built by the Emperor Constantine in the 4th century AD, after his mother Helen's pilgrimage to Palestine. The image of the Holy Land is captured by the Basilica of the Nativity, the site of the Birth of Jesus, and the Anastasis, the Basilica of the Holy Sepulchre, the site of the Resurrection. The hill of Golgotha behind the throne of Jesus separates the two basilicas, since the Death of Jesus occurs between the events of his Birth and his Resurrection. This amalgamation of buildings was Palestine as the early Christian pilgrims saw it. Their location in the background of this mosaic is a rich spiritual testimony to the dynamic connection between the Holy Land and Rome.

This beautiful apse mosaic is a fitting conclusion to this pilgrim's guidebook on Rome and the Holy Land. The Basilica of St. Pudenziana is located in Rome, and the mosaic, in part, symbolizes the Church of Rome by the two Apostles, St. Peter and St. Paul, who flank Christ and form a kind of triad of pastoral leadership. The Holy Land is illustrated in the mosaic by the motif of the architecture of the holy sites in Jerusalem and Bethlehem. The pilgrim's sacred geography of spiritual journey is encapsulated in this rich, multi-layered scene. The central focus is on Jesus, the Lord of history and the *Dominus Ecclesiae*, the Lord of the Church, as his scroll in the mosaic proclaims him.

Jesus Christ Is the Same Yesterday, Today, and Forever

The primary focus of the spirituality of pilgrimage in this book is the person of Jesus. The heart of the pilgrim, often dried out by the demands, pressures, and distractions of modern life, can be nourished and healed by the showered graces of the Lord of the journey. He is the one who speaks to the heart of the pilgrim by revealing himself as the journey unfolds. In this way, the trip of the pilgrim becomes a metaphor for the entire spiritual life. The faith of the pilgrim can deepen and expand during the pilgrimage, enabling one to embrace the spiritual challenges of daily life after the journey is over.

There is an old adage that says: "Pilgrims pass through the holy places, but the holy places pass through them." When sacred experiences, insights, impressions, and sites pass through the heart of the pilgrim, the inner landscape of faith is transformed and strengthened. May all those who use this guidebook find the courage to "open wide the doors to Christ," allowing him to shape the inner landscape of their hearts.

Stand beside the ancient roads, ask the pathways of old which is the way to good, and walk it; thus you will find rest for your souls (Jeremiah 6:16).

PHOTOGRAPHS

1. Pope John Paul II. Courtesy of New Diacolor, Rome, Italy.

2 Madaba Map. Courtesy of Biblical Archaeology Society.

3. Holy Door of St. Peter's basilica in Rome. Courtesy of author, Dr. Irena Vaisvilaite.

4. St. Peter's Square, courtesy of New Diacolor, Rome.

5. "Saint Veronica" by Hans Memling. National Gallery of Art, Washington, D.C. Courtesy of Edizione G. Quarta, Rome.

6. Fresco by Giotto of Pope Boniface VIII proclaiming first holy year, St. John Lateran, Rome. Courtesy of author, Dr. Irena Vaisvilaite.

7. "Veronica" by El Greco, Museum of Santa Cruz, Toldeo, Spain. Courtesy of Spanish Ministry of Culture.

8. Basilica of the Holy Sepulchre, Jerusalem. Courtesy of Holy Views, Ltd.

9. Fourth century AD marble profile of St. Peter and St. Paul, Paleo-Christian Museum, Aquileia, Italy. Courtesy of Tipolito Giusti, Rimini, Italy.

10. Dome of St. Peter's basilica, Rome. Courtesy of New Diacolor, Rome.

11. "Sacred Way" from the Roman Forum, Rome, Italy. Courtesy of New Diacolor, Rome.

12. Old City of Jerusalem as seen from the Mount of Olives. Courtesy of Holy Views, Ltd.

13. Golden Gate, Jerusalem. Courtesy of Biblical Archaeology Society.

14. Chapel of the Ascension, Mt. Of Olives, Jerusalem. Courtesy of Biblical Archaeology Society.

15. Panoramic of Jerusalem from the Church of Dominus Flevit, Mt. of Olives, Jerusalem. Courtesy of author, Dr. Irena Vaisvilaite.

16. Church of All Nations, Mt. of Olives, Jerusalem. Courtesy of Holy Views, Ltd.

17. The Garden of Gethsemane, Mt. of Olives, Jerusalem. Courtesy of Biblical Archaeology Society.

18. The Cenacle Room of the Last Supper, Jerusalem. Courtesy of Biblical Archaeology Society.

19. The Basilica of the Holy Sepulchre, Calvary altar, Courtesy of Holy Views, Ltd.

20. The Basilica of the Holy Sepulchre, Entrance to the Tomb of Jesus, Courtesy of Holy Views, Ltd.

21. Basilica of the Nativity, Bethlehem. Courtesy of Biblical Archaeology Society.

22. Twelfth century AD gilt mosaic above columns central nave of Basilica of Nativity. Courtesy of author Dr. Irena Vaisvilaite.

23. Interior of Basilica of Nativity, Bethlehem. Courtesy of Biblical Archaeology Society.

24. The Cave of the Nativity, Bethlehem. Courtesy of Biblical Archaeology Society.

25. Panoramic view of Nazareth. Courtesy of Holy Views, Ltd.

26. Basilica of Annunciation, Nazareth. Courtesy of Biblical Archaeology Society.

27 Roman Forum, Rome, Italy. Courtesy of author Dr. Irena Vaisvilaite.

28. Interior of Catacombs of St. Sebastian, Rome, Italy. Courtesy of author, Dr. Irena Vaisvilaite.

29. Pilgrims Map from the book, Seven Churches of Christian Rome, by Antonio Lafrery, 1575AD. Courtesy of Centro di Studi sulla cultura e l'immagine di Roma, Rome, Italy.

30. Incision of St. Peter and St. Paul displaying the Veronica image, by S. Torello from the book Libro di Buona Compagnia, 1577AD. Courtesy of Centro di Studi sulla cultura e l'immagine di Roma, Rome, Italy.

31. Fifth century AD mosaic of "Hospitality of Abraham" from interior of Basilica of St. Mary Major, Rome Italy. Courtesy of Basilica di Santa Maria Maggiore, Rome, Italy.

32. Interior of Basilica of St. Peter. Courtesy of author Dr. Irena Vaisvilaite.

33. Bridge of the Angels, Rome, Italy. Courtesy of author Dr. Irena Vaisvilaite.

34. St. Peter's Square. Courtesy of New Diacolor, Rome.

35. Baldacchino of St. Peter's. Courtesy of author Dr. Irena Vaisvilaite.

36. Statue of St. Peter, Basilica of St. Peter. Courtesy of author Dr. Irena Vaisvilaite.

37. Pallium Niche. Courtesy of Reverenda Fabbrica di S. Pietro, Vatican City.

38. Statue of St. Veronica, Basilica of St. Peter. Courtesy of author Dr. Irena Vaisvilaite.

39. Chair of Peter, Cathedra Petri, by Bernini, Basilica of St. Peter. Courtesy of author Dr. Irena Vaisvilaite.

PHOTOGRAPHS

❦

40. Basilica of St. Paul, Rome. Courtesy of New Diacolor, Rome.

41 Copy of the marble slab cover over the tomb of St. Paul., Pinacoteca Museum, Basilica of St. Paul Outside the Walls. Courtesy of author Dr. Aurelie A. Hagstrom.

42. Façade of Basilica of St. John Lateran and Statue of St. Francis of Assisi, Rome, Italy. Courtesy of New Diacolor, Rome.

43. Interior of Basilica of St. John Lateran. Courtesy of New Diacolor, Rome.

44. Apse mosaic of Basilica of St. John Lateran, Rome. Courtesy of author Dr. Irena Vaisvilaite.

45. Holy Stairs, Scala Sancta, Rome. Courtesy of author Dr. Irena Vaisvilaite.

46. Exterior of Basilica of St. Mary Major, Rome. Courtesy of author Dr. Irena Vaisvilaite.

47. Interior of Basilica of St. Mary Major. Courtesy of Basilica di Santa Maria Maggiore, Rome, Italy.

48. Apse Mosaic, Basilica of St. Mary Major, Rome. Courtesy of Basilica di Santa Maria Maggiore, Rome, Italy.

49. Ninth century AD Byzantine icon entitled: Salus Populi Romani, from the Pauline Chapel, Basilica of St. Mary Major, Rome. Courtesy of Basilica di Santa Maria Maggiore, Rome, Italy.

50. Fourth century AD apse mosaic, Basilica of St. Pudenziana, Rome. Courtesy of Basilica di Santa Pudenziana, Rome.

INDEX